Everyman's Poetry

Everyman, I will go with thee,
and be thy guide

Henry Wadsworth Longfellow

Selected and edited by ANTHONY THWAITE

D1530326

EVERYMAN

J. M. Dent · London

Introduction and other critical apparatus
© J. M. Dent 1996

J. M. Dent
Orion Publishing Group
Orion House
5 Upper St Martin's Lane
London WC2H 9EA

Typeset by Deltatype Ltd, Ellesmere Port, Cheshire
Printed in Great Britain by
The Guernsey Press Co. Ltd, Guernsey, C.I.

British Library Cataloguing-in-Publication
Data is available upon request.

ISBN 0 460 87821 2

Contents

Note on the Author and Editor

HENRY WADSWORTH LONGFELLOW (1807–82) was born in Portland, Maine (then part of the Commonwealth of Massachusetts), the son of a prosperous lawyer. He graduated from Bowdoin College in 1825 and was immediately offered a newly established professorship of modern languages there, to be taken up after a period of study in Europe, at his family's expense. Sailing for France in 1826, at the age of nineteen, he spent three years improving his French, German, Spanish and Italian. Back in America, he began work at Bowdoin and in 1831 married Mary Potter, the daughter of another Portland lawyer.

In the next few years he published his first books, one of them a prose account of his travels. He was offered the Smith Professorship of French and Spanish at Harvard, to be preceded by another visit to Europe. Early in 1835 he sailed for Germany. But in Holland his wife had a miscarriage, and she died in Rotterdam towards the end of that year.

It was when he was recuperating from this blow that in 1836 he met the woman who was to become his second wife, Frances (Fanny) Appleton, in Switzerland. But it was seven years before they married. Longfellow returned to Harvard and began teaching. Meanwhile, he published his first collection of original poems, *Voices of the Night*, in 1839: this book contains 'A Psalm of Life'. His enormous popular success began with the publication of *Evangeline* in 1847; but it was not until 1854, when he was forty-seven, that he felt confident enough to resign his Harvard professorship and live solely by his writing.

In the year he left Harvard, he read a German translation of a Finnish folk-epic which inspired him to write his own 'Indian Edda', *The Song of Hiawatha* (1855). He followed this in 1858 with *The Courtship of Miles Standish*. But in 1861 he suffered the worst blow in his life, when his wife Fanny died as a result of a domestic fire. Longfellow himself was badly burned.

In the last twenty years of his life, when his reputation seemed assured but when he was often deeply depressed, he wrote most of his best short poems. The last of his many books to be published in his lifetime was the two-volume *Ultima Thule* (1880–82).

ANTHONY THWAITE was born in 1930 in England. He spent the years 1940–44 as a wartime evacuee in the USA. After graduating from Christ Church, Oxford, in 1955, he lectured in English literature at Tokyo University for two years. Since then he has been a BBC radio producer, literary editor in turn of the *Listener* and the *New Statesman* and co-editor of *Encounter* 1973–85. He has also taught in universities in Libya, Britain and the United States. He has published many books of poetry, most recently *The Dust of the World* (1994), and several books of criticism and anthologies. He is a Fellow of the Royal Society of Literature, and in 1990 was awarded the OBE for services to poetry.

In 1993 he edited a more substantial Longfellow *Selected Poems* for the Everyman series.

Chronology of Longfellow's Life

Year	Life
1807	Longfellow born
1825	Graduates from Bowdoin College
1826–9	Longfellow in France, Spain and Germany
1831	Marries Mary Potter
1834	Offered Smith Professorship at Harvard
1835–6	Second journey to Europe; Mary dies in Rotterdam, November 1835
1839	Longfellow's first collection of poems, *Voices of the Night*, published a few months after his novel *Hyperion*
1843	Marries Fanny Appleton. Publishes his play *The Spanish Student*
1847	*Evangeline* and his novel *Kavanagh* published

Chronology of his Times

Year	Artistic Events	Historical Events
1807	Byron, *Hours of Idleness* Charles and Mary Lamb, *Tales from Shakespeare*	US Congress passes the Embargo Act, stopping all foreign trade; President Jefferson takes initiative in banning importation of any more slaves from Africa
1825		John Quincy Adams elected President of United States; Peru and Bolivia declare independence from Spain; world's first steam railway opens in England (Stockton to Darlington)
1826–9	Tennyson's first book published, 1827 Deaths of Beethoven and William Blake, 1827 Death of Schubert, 1828	
1831		Nat Turner, rebel slave, hanged
1834	Death of Coleridge	Slavery abolished in British colonies
1835–6	Browning, *Paracelsus*, 1835 Dickens, *Sketches by Boz*, 1836	Mexican troops storm Alamo in Texas, 1836
1843	Wordsworth made Poet Laureate	
1847	Tennyson, *The Princess* Charlotte Brontë, *Jane Eyre* Emily Brontë, *Wuthering Heights*	US Army storms Mexico City; Marx's *Communist Manifesto* published

Year	Life
1848	Publishes *Poems, Lyrical and Dramatic*
1854	Resigns from Harvard
1855	*The Song of Hiawatha* published
1861	Death of Fanny Longfellow in fire
1868	*Poetical Works* published
1872	Second volume of *Poetical Works* published
1880	Publishes first volume of *Ultima Thule*
1882	Publishes second volume of *Ultima Thule*. Dies 24 March

Year	Artistic Events	Historical Events
1848	Death of Emily Brontë	Rebellions and uprisings in France, Italy, Austria, Hungary etc; Mexico cedes Texas and California to United States
1854		Light Brigade wiped out at Balaclava
1855	Whitman, *Leaves of Grass* Tennyson, *Maud and Other Poems*	French and British capture Sebastopol
1861	Deaths of Elizabeth Barrett Browning and Clough	Outbreak of American Civil War
1868	Robert Browning, *The Ring and the Book* Louisa May Alcott, *Little Women* Wilkie Collins, *The Moonstone*	Emperor Meiji restored to power in Japan, after two centuries of rule by the Tokugawa Shogunate
1872	Samuel Butler, *Erewhon* Thomas Hardy, *Under the Greenwood Tree*	Drought and Stock Exchange panic in the United States
1880	Death of George Eliot	British troops lift siege of Kandahar in Afghanistan; Ned Kelly executed in Australia
1882	Death of Emerson	British defeat Egyptians at Tel el-Kebir

Introduction

For many years during his life and for some time afterwards, Longfellow was thought to be a great writer in both America and Britain. He was widely regarded as not only the glory of American letters but was also loved as one of the greatest poets of the English language itself. But within forty or so years after his death in 1882 he had become an object of derision. After that, there has not even been derision, simply neglect.

Some of the reasons for both derision and neglect are not hard to find. An age without illusions, and also without religious faith, found the bracing moral exhortations of 'A Psalm of Life' fatuously simple-minded. The long verse narratives – *Evangeline*, *The Courtship of Miles Standish*, *The Song of Hiawatha* – outstayed their welcome in an era in which the prose novel seemed utterly to have taken over that story-telling function. The Modernism of T. S. Eliot and Ezra Pound had no use for such things. More recently, the increasing professionalisation of the academic study of literature saw that there was little 'work' to be done on Longfellow. His poetry was straightforward: it did not need to be teased out, delved into, explained. Longfellow failed to be difficult, and he often succeeded in being tedious.

There are some truths in this, but it is not the whole truth. If we look carefully at Longfellow's poems in the context of the fifty-odd years in which they were produced, we can see that he was in some ways a pioneer – in his use of the English hexameter in *Evangeline*, in his even more daring use of the trochaic tetrameter in *Hiawatha*. But technical innovation in itself doesn't necessarily sustain long-lasting interest: the technical innovations of, say, Emily Dickinson or Gerard Manley Hopkins don't in themselves account for the fact that they are read when Longfellow is not.

It is in the shorter poem – the elegy, the meditation, the pregnant lyric, the sonnet, the epitaph – that Longfellow still deserves to be read: not, perhaps, as a great poet (in the way we can still call his contemporaries Tennyson and Browning great), but as a very accomplished, skilful, thoughtful and honest minor poet. At his best his poems of mortality, loss and disappointment are as moving as all but the best by Tennyson and Hardy.

Out of his grief at the accidental death of his second wife came 'The Cross of Snow':

> Such is the cross I wear upon my breast
> These eighteen years, through all the changing scenes
> And seasons, changeless since the day she died.

The poems which, in his old age, drew on memories of his childhood on the New England coast are often as fine: 'Four by the Clock', 'Chimes', 'Becalmed', the Dedication of his book of poems *Ultima Thule*, and, most piercingly, 'My Lost Youth' (from which Robert Frost took his title *A Boy's Will*) and the magnificent 'The Tide Rises, the Tide Falls', one of the finest lyrics in English.

I would add to these some of the sonnets 'On Translating the Divina Commedia,' 'The Fire of Drift-Wood', 'Haunted Houses', 'In the Churchyard at Cambridge', 'The Two Angels', 'The Jewish Cemetery at Newport' and 'Aftermath'. Perhaps the most unjustly treated of all is the sonnet 'Nature'. Of this, one of Longfellow's more appreciative and acute modern critics, Newton Arvin, commented that it is one of his 'distinctly inferior poems'; while another American critic, Bruce Kellner, though granting that it 'ends superbly', writes about its 'insufferable circuitous dependent clause taking up all of its octet'. On the contrary, I find the control of the long simile throughout both the sections of this sonnet a marvellous technical achievement, and the phrasing and cadences deeply moving. The poem's quiet confidence achieves an *adagio*-like effect which reverberates and haunts me whenever I read it or remember it.

At the very least, Longfellow was an adept and alert craftsman who tried many forms as well as many subjects. Some of what he wrote probably cannot be resurrected, for the reasons I have suggested. We often see him through the wrong eyes or, more often, listen to him with the wrong ears. It is of course difficult, perhaps impossible, to read *Hiawatha* with ears that have not been blunted by the relentless noise of parodies, most famously Lewis Carroll's cheeky 'Hiawatha's Photographing', written just two years after the poem it parodies. If *Hiawatha* is read monotonously, it will sound monotonous. But it need not be so. Certainly the measure itself is not irretrievable for serious purposes: a century and a quarter later, Philip Larkin somehow found himself using it, very effectively, in his haunting poem 'The Explosion'. In this present selection, I have chosen just three complete extracts from the twenty-two which make up the whole; but *The Song of Hiawatha* can be found *in toto* in the longer *Selected Poems* I edited for Everyman in 1993, and it can also be found as a separate volume in the Everyman series.

Evangeline and *The Courtship of Miles Standish* are much more resistant long poems from which to take extracts, and I have neglected them here: both can be found in my 1993 *Selected Poems*. What I have tried to do in this present book is to concentrate on the best of the shorter pieces, as well as on a handful of once-famous (or notorious) poems, such as 'A Psalm of Life' and 'The Village Blacksmith'. I think that the only hoary old favourite that I jibbed at – and therefore have finally excluded – is 'Excelsior'.

I believe that enough remains which is lively, stirring, moving and true for anyone who has not become blind to a well-made poem to find pleasure in reading Longfellow, in selection if not in bulk (and he was a formidably prolific poet). For all the fame and honours that came to him in his lifetime, he was never sure of his own merit: one has only to read 'Mezzo Cammin' to see this. He wrote it (as his headnote makes clear) comparatively early on, in 1842, but did not publish it in his lifetime. In it, he lamented what he had not managed to achieve, and heard a pre-echo of the remorseless future:

> on the autumnal blast
> The cataract of Death far thundering from the heights.

Worse poets have felt more confident of themselves, and of posterity, than Longfellow. He was never smug, he was never dishonest in his work or, as far as one can see, in his life. He deserves much better than his present dubious position in the shadows of literary history.

ANTHONY THWAITE

Henry Wadsworth Longfellow

A Psalm of Life

What the heart of the young man
said to the psalmist

Tell me not, in mournful numbers,
    'Life is but an empty dream!'
For the soul is dead that slumbers,
    And things are not what they seem.

Life is real! Life is earnest!
    And the grave is not its goal;
'Dust thou art, to dust returnest,'
    Was not spoken of the soul.

Not enjoyment, and not sorrow,
    Is our destined end or way;
But to act, that each to-morrow
    Finds us farther than to-day.

Art is long, and Time is fleeting,
    And our hearts, though stout and brave,
Still, like muffled drums, are beating
    Funeral marches to the grave.

In the world's broad field of battle,
    In the bivouac of Life,
Be not like dumb, driven cattle!
    Be a hero in the strife!

Trust no Future, howe'er pleasant!
    Let the dead Past bury its dead!
Act, – act in the living Present!
    Heart within, and God o'erhead!

Lives of great men all remind us
    We can make our lives sublime,

And, departing, leave behind us
    Footprints on the sands of time;

Footprints, that perhaps another,
    Sailing o'er life's solemn main,
A forlorn and shipwrecked brother,
    Seeing, shall take heart again.

Let us, then, be up and doing,
    With a heart for any fate;
Still achieving, still pursuing,
    Learn to labour and to wait.

The Reaper and the Flowers

There is a Reaper, whose name is Death,
    And, with his sickle keen,
He reaps the bearded grain at a breath,
    And the flowers that grow between.

'Shall I have nought that is fair?' saith he,
    'Have nought but the bearded grain?
Though the breath of these flowers is sweet to me,
    I will give them all back again.'

He gazed at the flowers with tearful eyes,
    He kissed their drooping leaves;
It was for the Lord of Paradise
    He bound them in his sheaves.

'My Lord has need of these flowerets gay,'
    The Reaper said, and smiled;
'Dear tokens of the earth are they,
    Where he was once a child.

'They shall all bloom in fields of light,
    Transplanted by my care,
And saints, upon their garments white,
    These sacred blossoms wear.'

And the mother gave, in tears and pain,
    The flowers she most did love;
She knew she should find them all again,
    In the fields of light above.

O, not in cruelty, not in wrath,
    The Reaper came that day;
'Twas an angel visited the green earth,
    And took the flowers away.

The Light of Stars

The night is come, but not too soon;
   And sinking silently,
All silently, the little moon
   Drops down behind the sky.

There is no light in earth or heaven,
   But the cold light of stars;
And the first watch of night is given
   To the red planet Mars.

Is it the tender star of love?
   The star of love and dreams?
O no! from that blue tent above,
   A hero's armour gleams.

And earnest thoughts within me rise,
   When I behold afar,
Suspended in the evening skies,
   The shield of that red star.

O star of strength! I see thee stand
   And smile upon my pain;
Thou beckonest with thy mailed hand,
   And I am strong again.

Within my breast there is no light,
   But the cold light of stars;
I give the first watch of the night
   To the red planet Mars.

The star of the unconquered will,
   He rises in my breast,
Serene, and resolute, and still,
   And calm, and self-possessed.

And thou, too, whosoe'er thou art,
   That readest this brief psalm,

As one by one thy hopes depart,
  Be resolute and calm.

O fear not in a world like this,
  And thou shalt know ere long,
Know how sublime a thing it is
  To suffer and be strong.

Burial of the Minnisink

On sunny slope and beechen swell,
The shadowed light of evening fell;
And, where the maple's leaf was brown,
With soft and silent lapse came down
The glory, that the wood receives,
At sunset, in its brazen leaves.

Far upward in the mellow light
Rose the blue hills. One cloud of white,
Around a far uplifted cone,
In the warm blush of evening shone;
An image of the silver lakes,
By which the Indian's soul awakes.

But soon a funeral hymn was heard
Where the soft breath of evening stirred
The tall, gray forest; and a band
Of stern in heart, and strong in hand,
Came winding down beside the wave,
To lay the red chief in his grave.

They sang, that by his native bowers
He stood, in the last moon of flowers,
And thirty snows had not yet shed
Their glory on the warrior's head;
But, as the summer fruit decays,
So died he in those naked days.

A dark cloak of the roebuck's skin
Covered the warrior, and within
Its heavy folds the weapons, made
For the hard toils of war, were laid;
The cuirass, woven of plaited reeds,
And the broad belt of shells and beads.

Before, a dark-haired virgin train
Chanted the death dirge of the slain;

Behind, the long procession came
Of hoary men and chiefs of fame,
With heavy hearts, and eyes of grief,
Leading the war-horse of their chief.

Stripped of his proud and martial dress,
Uncurbed, unreined, and riderless,
With darting eye, and nostril spread,
And heavy and impatient tread,
He came; and oft that eye so proud
Asked for his rider in the crowd.

They buried the dark chief, they freed
Beside the grave his battle steed;
And swift an arrow cleaved its way
To his stern heart! One piercing neigh
Arose, – and, on the dead man's plain,
The rider grasps his steed again.

The Indian Hunter

When the summer harvest was gather'd in,
And the sheaf of the gleaner grew white and thin,
And the ploughshare was in its furrow left,
Where the stubble land had been lately cleft,
An Indian hunter, with unstrung bow,
Look'd down where the valley lay stretch'd below.

He was a stranger there, and all that day,
Had been out on the hills, a perilous way,
But the foot of the deer was far and fleet,
And the wolf kept aloof from the hunter's feet,
And bitter feelings pass'd o'er him then,
As he stood by the populous haunts of men.

The winds of autumn came over the woods
As the sun stole out from their solitudes,
The moss was white on the maple's trunk,
And dead from its arms the pale vine shrunk,
And ripen'd the mellow fruit hung, and red
Were the tree's wither'd leaves round it shed.

The foot of the reaper moved slow on the lawn,
And the sickle cut down the yellow corn, –
The mower sung loud by the meadow-side,
Where the mists of evening were spreading wide,
And the voice of the herdsman came up the lea,
And the dance went round by the greenwood tree.

Then the hunter turn'd away from that scene,
Where the home of his fathers once had been,
And heard by the distant and measured stroke,
That the woodman hew'd down the giant oak,
And burning thoughts flash'd over his mind,
Of the white man's faith, and love unkind.

The moon of the harvest grew high and bright,
As her golden horn pierced the cloud of white, –

A footstep was heard in the rustling brake,
Where the beech overshadow'd the misty lake,
And a mourning voice, and a plunge from the shore; –
And the hunter was seen on the hills no more.

When years had pass'd on, by that still lake-side
The fisher look'd down through the silver tide,
And there on the smooth yellow sand display'd,
A skeleton wasted and white was laid,
And 'twas seen, as the waters moved deep and slow,
That the hand was still grasping a hunter's bow.

The Wreck of the Hesperus

It was the schooner Hesperus,
    That sailed the wintry sea;
And the skipper had taken his little daughtèr,
    To bear him company.

Blue were her eyes as the fairy-flax,
    Her cheeks like the dawn of day,
And her bosom white as the hawthorn buds
    That ope in the month of May.

The skipper he stood beside the helm,
    His pipe was in his mouth,
And he watched how the veering flaw did blow
    The smoke now West, now South.

Then up and spake an old Sailòr,
    Had sailed the Spanish Main,
'I pray thee, put into yonder port,
    For I fear a hurricane.

'Last night the moon had a golden ring,
    And to-night no moon we see!'
The skipper he blew a whiff from his pipe,
    And a scornful laugh laughed he.

Colder and colder blew the wind,
    A gale from the North-east;
The snow fell hissing in the brine,
    And the billows frothed like yeast.

Down came the storm, and smote amain,
    The vessel in its strength;
She shuddered and paused, like a frightened steed,
    Then leaped her cable's length.

'Come hither! come hither! my little daughtèr,
    And do not tremble so;

For I can weather the roughest gale,
   That ever wind did blow.'

He wrapped her warm in his seaman's coat
   Against the stinging blast;
He cut a rope from a broken spar,
   And bound her to the mast.

'O father! I hear the church-bells ring,
   O say, what may it be?'
' 'Tis a fog-bell on a rock-bound coast!' –
   And he steered for the open sea.

'O father! I hear the sound of guns,
   O say, what may it be?'
'Some ship in distress, that cannot live
   In such an angry sea!'

'O father! I see a gleaming light,
   O say, what may it be?'
But the father answered never a word,
   A frozen corpse was he.

Lashed to the helm, all stiff and stark,
   With his face turned to the skies,
The lantern gleamed through the gleaming snow
   On his fixed and glassy eyes.

Then the maiden clasped her hands and prayed
   That savèd she might be;
And she thought of Christ, who stilled the wave,
   On the Lake of Galilee.

And fast through the midnight dark and drear,
   Through the whistling sleet and snow,
Like a sheeted ghost, the vessel swept
   Towards the reef of Norman's Woe.

And ever the fitful gusts between
   A sound came from the land;

It was the sound of the trampling surf,
   On the rocks and the hard sea-sand.

The breakers were right beneath her bows,
   She drifted a dreary wreck,
And a whooping billow swept the crew
   Like icicles from her deck.

She struck where the white and fleecy waves
   Looked soft as carded wool,
But the cruel rocks, they gored her side
   Like the horns of an angry bull.

Her rattling shrouds, all sheathed in ice,
   With the masts went by the board;
Like a vessel of glass, she stove and sank,
   Ho! ho! the breakers roared!

At daybreak, on the bleak sea-beach,
   A fisherman stood aghast,
To see the form of a maiden fair,
   Lashed close to a drifting mast.

The salt sea was frozen on her breast,
   The salt tears in her eyes;
And he saw her hair, like the brown sea-weed,
   On the billows fall and rise.

Such was the wreck of the Hesperus,
   In the midnight and the snow!
Christ save us all from a death like this
   On the reef of Norman's Woe!

The Song of Hiawatha

Introduction

Should you ask me, whence these stories?
Whence these legends and traditions,
With the odours of the forest,
With the dew and damp of meadows,
With the curling smoke of wigwams,
With the rushing of great rivers,
With their frequent repetitions,
And their wild reverberations,
As of thunder in the mountains?
   I should answer, I should tell you,
'From the forests and the prairies,
From the great lakes of the North-land,
From the land of the Ojibways,
From the land of the Dakotahs,
From the mountains, moors, and fen-lands,
Where the heron, and Shuh-shuh-gah,
Feeds among the reeds and rushes.
I repeat them as I heard them
From the lips of Nawadaha,
The musician, the sweet singer.'
   Should you ask where Nawadaha
Found these songs, so wild and wayward,
Found these legends and traditions,
I should answer, I should tell you,
'In the bird's-nests of the forest,
In the lodges of the beaver,
In the hoof-prints of the bison,
In the eyrie of the eagle!
'All the wild-fowl sang them to him,
In the moorlands and the fen-lands,
In the melancholy marshes;
Chetowaik, the plover, sang them,

Mahng, the loon, the wild-goose,
   Wawa,
The blue heron, the Shuh-shuh-gah,
And the grouse, the Mushkodasa!'
   If still further you should ask me
Saying, 'Who was Nawadaha?
Tell us of this Nawadaha,'
I should answer your inquiries
Straightway in such words as follow:
   In the Vale of Tawasentha,
In the green and silent valley,
By the pleasant watercourses,
Dwelt the singer Nawadaha.
Round about the Indian village
Spread the meadows and the corn-fields,
And beyond them stood the forest,
Stood the groves of the singing pine-trees,
Green in Summer, white in Winter,
Ever sighing, ever singing.
   'And the pleasant watercourses,
You could trace them through the valley,
By the rushing in the Spring-time,
By the alders in the Summer,
By the white fog in the Autumn,
By the black line in the Winter;
And beside them dwelt the singer,
In the vale of Tawasentha,
In the green and silent valley.
   'There he sang of Hiawatha,
Sang the Song of Hiawatha,
Sang his wondrous birth and being,
How he prayed and how he fasted,
How he lived, and toiled, and suffered,
That the tribes of men might prosper,
That he might advance his people!'
   Ye who love the haunts of Nature,
Love the sunshine of the meadow,
Love the shadow of the forest,
Love the wind among the branches,

And the rain-shower and the snow-storm,
And the rushing of great rivers
Through their palisades of pine-trees,
And the thunder in the mountains,
Whose innumerable echoes
Flap like eagles in their eyries; –
Listen to these wild traditions,
To this Song of Hiawatha!

Ye who love a nation's legends,
Love the ballads of a people,
That like voices from afar off
Waving like a hand that beckons,
Call to us to pause and listen,
Speak in tones so plain and child-like,
Scarcely can the ear distinguish
Whether they are sung or spoken; –
Listen to this Indian Legend,
To this Song of Hiawatha!

Ye whose hearts are fresh and simple,
Who have faith in God and Nature,
Who believe, that in all ages
Every human heart is human,
That in even savage bosoms
There are longings, yearnings, strivings
For the good they comprehend not,
That the feeble hands and helpless,
Groping blindly in the darkness,
Touch God's right hand in that darkness
And are lifted up and strengthened; –
Listen to this simple story,
To this Song of Hiawatha!

Ye, who sometimes in your rambles
Through the green lanes of the country,
Where the tangled barberry-bushes
Hang their tufts of crimson berries
Over stone walls gray with mosses,
Pause by some neglected grave-yard,
For a while to muse, and ponder
On a half-effaced inscription,

Written with little skill of song-craft,
Homely phrases, but each letter
Full of hope, and yet of heart-break,
Full of all the tender pathos
Of the Here and the Hereafter; –
Stay and read this rude inscription,
Read this Song of Hiawatha!

Hiawatha's Wooing

'As unto the bow the cord is,
So unto the man is woman,
Though she bends him, she obeys him,
Though she draws him, yet she follows,
Useless each without the other!'
  Thus the youthful Hiawatha
Said within himself and pondered,
Much perplexed by various feelings,
Listless, longing, hoping, fearing,
Dreaming still of Minnehaha,
Of the lovely Laughing Water,
In the land of the Dacotahs.
'Wed a maiden of your people,'
Warning said the old Nokomis;
'Go not eastward, go not westward,
For a stranger, whom we know not!
Like a fire upon the hearthstone
Is a neighbour's homely daughter,
Like the starlight or the moonlight
Is the handsomest of strangers!'
  Thus dissuading spake Nokomis,
And my Hiawatha answered
Only this: 'Dear old Nokomis,
Very pleasant is the firelight,
But I like the starlight better,
Better do I like the moonlight!'
  Gravely then said old Nokomis:

'Bring not here an idle maiden,
Bring not here a useless woman,
Hands unskilful, feet unwilling;
Bring a wife with nimble fingers,
Heart and hand that move together,
Feet that run on willing errands!'
    Smiling answered Hiawatha;
'In the land of the Dacotahs
Lives the Arrow-maker's daughter,
Minnehaha, Laughing Water,
Handsomest of all the women.
I will bring her to your wigwam,
She shall run upon your errands,
Be your starlight, moonlight, firelight,
Be the sunlight of my people!'
    Still dissuading said Nokomis:
'Bring not to my lodge a stranger
From the land of the Dacotahs!
Very fierce are the Dacotahs,
Often is there war between us,
There are feuds yet unforgotten,
Wounds that ache and still may open!'
    Laughing answered Hiawatha:
'For that reason, if no other,
Would I wed the fair Dacotah,
That our tribes might be united,
That old feuds might be forgotten,
And old wounds be healed for ever!'
    Thus departed Hiawatha
To the land of the Dacotahs,
To the land of handsome women;
Striding over moor and meadow,
Through interminable forests,
Through uninterrupted silence.
    With his moccasins of magic,
At each stride a mile he measured;
Yet the way seemed long before him,
And his heart outrun his footsteps;
And he journeyed without resting,
Till he heard the cataract's thunder,

Heard the Falls of Minnehaha,
Calling to him through the silence.
'Pleasant is the sound!' he murmured,
'Pleasant is the voice that calls me!'
   On the outskirts of the forest,
'Twixt the shadow and the sunshine,
Herds of fallow deer were feeding,
But they saw not Hiawatha;
To his bow he whispered, 'Fail not!'
To his arrow whispered, 'Swerve not!'
Sent it singing on its errand,
To the red heart of the roebuck;
Threw the deer across his shoulder,
And sped forward without pausing.
   At the doorway of his wigwam
Sat the ancient Arrow-maker,
In the land of the Dacotahs,
Making arrow-heads of jasper,
Arrow-heads of chalcedony.
At his side, in all her beauty,
Sat the lovely Minnehaha,
Sat his daughter, Laughing Water,
Plaiting mats of flags and rushes;
Of the past the old man's thoughts were,
And the maiden's of the future.
   He was thinking, as he sat there,
Of the days when with such arrows
He had struck the deer and bison,
On the Muskoday, the meadow;
Shot the wild goose, flying southward,
On the wing, the clamorous Wawa;
Thinking of the great war-parties,
How they came to buy his arrows,
Could not fight without his arrows.
Ah, no more such noble warriors
Could be found on earth as they were!
Now the men were all like women,
Only used their tongues for weapons!
   She was thinking of a hunter,
From another tribe and country,

Young and tall and very handsome,
Who one morning, in the Springtime,
Came to buy her father's arrows,
Sat and rested in the wigwam,
Lingered long about the doorway,
Looking back as he departed.
She had heard her father praise him,
Praise his courage and his wisdom;
Would he come again for arrows
To the Falls of Minnehaha?
On the mat her hands lay idle,
And her eyes were very dreamy.

Through their thoughts they heard a footstep,
Heard a rustling in the branches,
And with glowing cheek and forehead,
With the deer upon his shoulders,
Suddenly from out the woodlands
Hiawatha stood before them.

Straight the ancient Arrowmaker
Looked up gravely from his labour,
Laid aside the unfinished arrow,
Bade him enter at the doorway,
Saying, as he rose to meet him,
'Hiawatha, you are welcome!'

At the feet of Laughing Water
Hiawatha laid his burden,
Threw the red deer from his shoulders;
And the maiden looked up at him,
Looked up from her mat of rushes,
Said with gentle look and accent,
'You are welcome, Hiawatha!'

Very spacious was the wigwam,
Made of deerskin dressed and whitened,
With the Gods of the Dacotahs
Drawn and painted on its curtains,
And so tall the doorway, hardly
Hiawatha stooped to enter,
Hardly touched his eagle-feathers
As he entered at the doorway.

Then uprose the Laughing Water,

From the ground fair Minnehaha,
Lay aside her mat unfinished,
Brought forth food and set before them,
Water brought them from the brooklet,
Gave them food in earthen vessels,
Gave them drink in bowls of basswood,
Listened while the guest was speaking,
Listened while her father answered,
But not once her lips she opened,
Not a single word she uttered.

Yes, as in a dream she listened
To the words of Hiawatha,
As he talked of old Nokomis,
Who had nursed him in his childhood,
As he told of his companions,
Chibiabos, the musician,
And the very strong man, Kwasind,
And of happiness and plenty
In the land of the Ojibways,
In the pleasant land and peaceful.

'After many years of warfare,
Many years of strife and bloodshed,
There is peace between the Ojibways
And the tribe of the Dacotahs.'
Thus continued Hiawatha,
And then added, speaking slowly,
'That this peace may last for ever,
And our hands be clasped more closely,
And our hearts be more united,
Give me as my wife this maiden,
Minnehaha, Laughing Water,
Loveliest of Dacotah women!'

And the ancient Arrow-maker
Paused a moment ere he answered,
Smoked a little while in silence,
Looked at Hiawatha proudly,
Fondly looked at Laughing Water,
And made answer very gravely:
'Yes, if Minnehaha wishes;
Let your heart speak, Minnehaha!'

And the lovely Laughing Water
Seemed more lovely, as she stood there,
Neither willing nor reluctant,
As she went to Hiawatha,
Softly took the seat beside him,
While she said, and blushed to say it,
'I will follow you, my husband!'
    This was Hiawatha's wooing!
Thus it was he won the daughter
Of the ancient Arrow-maker,
In the land of the Dacotahs!
    From the wigwam he departed,
Leading with him Laughing Water;
Hand in hand they went together,
Through the woodland and the meadow,
Left the old man standing lonely
At the doorway of his wigwam,
Heard the Falls of Minnehaha
Calling to them from the distance,
Crying to them from afar off,
'Fare thee well, O Minnehaha!'
    And the ancient Arrow-maker
Turned again unto his labour,
Sat down by his sunny doorway,
Murmuring to himself, and saying:
'Thus it is our daughters leave us,
Those we love, and those who love us!
Just when they have learned to help us,
When we are old and lean upon them,
Comes a youth with flaunting feathers,
With his flute of reeds, a stranger
Wanders piping through the village,
Beckons to the fairest maiden,
As she follows where he leads her,
Leaving all things for the stranger!'
    Pleasant was the journey homeward,
Through interminable forests,
Over meadow, over mountain,
Over river, hill, and hollow.
Short it seemed to Hiawatha,

Though they journeyed very slowly,
Though his pace he checked and slackened
To the steps of Laughing Water.
   Over wide and rushing rivers
In his arms he bore the maiden;
Light he thought her as a feather,
As the plume upon his headgear;
Cleared the tangled pathway for her,
Bent aside the swaying branches,
Made at night a lodge of branches,
And a bed with boughs of hemlock,
And a fire before the doorway
With the dry cones of the pine tree.
   All the travelling winds went with them,
O'er the meadow, through the forest;
All the stars of night looked at them,
Watched with sleepless eyes their slumber;
From his ambush in the oak tree
Peeped the squirrel, Adjidaumo,
Watched with eager eyes the lovers;
And the rabbit, the Wabasso,
Scampered from the path before them,
Peering, peeping from his burrow,
Sat erect upon his haunches,
Watched with curious eyes the lovers.
   Pleasant was the journey homeward!
All the birds sang loud and sweetly
Songs of happiness and heart's-ease;
Sang the bluebird, the Owaissa,
'Happy are you, Hiawatha,
Having such a wife to love you!'
Sang the Opechee, the robin,
'Happy are you, Laughing Water,
Having such a noble husband!'
   From the sky the sun benignant
Looked upon them through the branches,
Saying to them, 'O my children,
Love is sunshine, hate is shadow,
Life is checkered shade and sunshine,
Rule by love, O Hiawatha!'

From the sky the moon looked at them,
Filled the lodge with mystic splendours,
Whispered to them, 'O my children,
Day is restless, night is quiet,
Man imperious, woman feeble;
Half is mine, although I follow;
Rule by patience, Laughing Water!'
    Thus it was they journeyed homeward;
Thus it was that Hiawatha
To the lodge of old Nokomis
Brought the moonlight, starlight, firelight,
Brought the sunshine of his people,
Minnehaha, Laughing Water,
Handsomest of all the women
In the land of the Dacotahs,
In the land of handsome women.

The Famine

O the long and dreary Winter!
O the cold and cruel Winter!
Ever thicker, thicker, thicker
Froze the ice on lake and river,
Ever deeper, deeper, deeper
Fell the snow o'er all the landscape,
Fell the covering snow, and drifted
Through the forest, round the village.
    Hardly from his buried wigwam
Could the hunter force a passage;
With his mittens and his snowshoes
Vainly walked he through the forest,
Sought for bird or beast and found none,
Saw no track of deer or rabbit,
In the snow beheld no footprints,
In the ghastly, gleaming forest
Fell, and could not rise from weakness,
Perished there from cold and hunger.

O the famine and the fever!
O the wasting of the famine!
O the blasting of the fever!
O the wailing of the children!
O the anguish of the women!
    All the earth was sick and famished;
Hungry was the air around them,
Hungry was the sky above them,
And the hungry stars in heaven
Like the eyes of wolves glared at them!
    Into Hiawatha's wigwam
Came two other guests, as silent
As the ghosts were, and as gloomy,
Waited not to be invited,
Did not parley at the doorway,
Sat there without word of welcome
In the seat of Laughing Water;
Looked with haggard eyes and hollow
At the face of Laughing Water.
    And the foremost said: 'Behold me!
I am Famine, Bukadawin!'
And the other said: 'Behold me!
I am Fever, Ahkosewin!'
    And the lovely Minnehaha
Shuddered as they looked upon her,
Shuddered at the words they uttered,
Lay down on her bed in silence,
Hid her face, but made no answer;
Lay there trembling, freezing, burning
At the looks they cast upon her,
At the fearful words they uttered.
    Forth into the empty forest
Rushed the maddened Hiawatha;
In his heart was deadly sorrow,
In his face a stony firmness;
On his brow the sweat of anguish
Started, but it froze and fell not.
    Wrapped in furs and armed for hunting,
With his mighty bow of ash-tree,
With his quiver full of arrows,

With his mittens, Minjekahwun,
Into the vast and vacant forest
On his snow-shoes strode he forward.
  'Gitche Manito, the Mighty!'
Cried he with his face uplifted
In that bitter hour of anguish,
'Give your children food, O father!
Give us food, or we must perish!
Give me food for Minnehaha,
For my dying Minnehaha!'
  Through the far-resounding forest,
Through the forest vast and vacant
Rang that cry of desolation.
But there came no other answer
Than the echo of his crying,
Than the echo of the woodlands,
'Minnehaha! Minnehaha!'
  All day long roved Hiawatha
In that melancholy forest,
Through the shadow of whose thickets,
In the pleasant days of Summer,
Of that ne'er forgotten Summer,
He had brought his young wife homeward
From the land of the Dacotahs;
When the birds sang in the thickets,
And the streamlets laughed and glistened,
And the air was full of fragrance,
And the lovely Laughing Water
Said with voice that did not tremble,
'I will follow you, my husband!'
In the wigwam with Nokomis,
With those gloomy guests, that watched her,
With the Famine and the Fever,
She was lying, the Beloved,
She the dying Minnehaha.
  'Hark!' she said; 'I hear a rushing,
Hear a roaring and a rushing,
Hear the Falls of Minnehaha
Calling to me from a distance!'
'No, my child!' said old Nokomis

''Tis the night-wind in the pine-trees!'
'Look!' she said; 'I see my father
Standing lonely at his doorway,
Beckoning to me from his wigwam
In the land of the Dacotahs!'
'No, my child!' said old Nokomis,
''Tis the smoke, that waves and beckons!'
    'Ah!' said she, 'the eyes of Pauguk
Glare upon me in the darkness,
I can feel his icy fingers
Clasping mine amid the darkness!
Hiawatha! Hiawatha!'
    And the desolate Hiawatha,
Far away amid the forest,
Miles away among the mountains,
Heard that sudden cry of anguish,
Heard the voice of Minnehaha
Calling to him in the darkness,
'Hiawatha! Hiawatha!'
    Over snowfields waste and pathless
Under snow-encumbered branches,
Homeward hurried Hiawatha,
Empty-handed, heavy-hearted,
Heard Nokomis moaning, wailing:
'Wahonowin! Wahonowin!
Would that I had perished for you,
Would that I were dead as you are!
Wahonowin! Wahonowin!'
    And he rushed into the wigwam,
Saw the old Nokomis slowly
Rocking to and fro and moaning,
Saw his lovely Minnehaha
Lying dead and cold before him,
And his bursting heart within him
Uttered such a cry of anguish,
That the forest moaned and shuddered,
That the very stars in heaven
Shook and trembled with his anguish.
    Then he sat down, still and speechless,
On the bed of Minnehaha,

At the feet of Laughing Water,
At those willing feet, that never
More would lightly run to meet him,
Never more would lightly follow.
   With both hands his face he covered,
Seven long days and nights he sat there,
As if in a swoon he sat there,
Speechless, motionless, unconscious
Of the daylight or the darkness.
   Then they buried Minnehaha;
In the snow a grave they made her,
In the forest deep and darksome,
Underneath the moaning hemlocks;
Clothed in her richest garments,
Wrapped in her robes of ermine;
Covered her with snow, like ermine,
Thus they buried Minnehaha.
   And at night a fire was lighted,
On her grave four times was kindled,
For her soul upon its journey
To the Islands of the Blessed.
From his doorway Hiawatha
Saw it burning in the forest,
Lighting up the gloomy hemlocks;
From his sleepless bed uprising,
From the bed of Minnehaha,
Stood and watched it at the doorway,
That it might not be extinguished,
Might not leave her in the darkness.
   'Farewell!' said he, 'Minnehaha!
Farewell, O my Laughing Water!
All my heart is buried with you,
All my thoughts go onward with you!
Come not back again to labour,
Come not back again to suffer,
Where the Famine and the Fever
Wear the heart and waste the body.
Soon my task will be completed,
Soon your footsteps I shall follow
To the Islands of the Blessed,

To the Kingdom of Ponemah,
To the Land of the Hereafter!'

The Village Blacksmith

Under a spreading chestnut tree
    The village smithy stands;
The smith, a mighty man is he,
    With large and sinewy hands;
And the muscles of his brawny arms
    Are strong as iron bands.

His hair is crisp, and black, and long,
    His face is like the tan;
His brow is wet with honest sweat,
    He earns whate'er he can,
And looks the whole world in the face,
    For he owes not any man.

Week in, week out, from morn till night,
    You can hear his bellows blow;
You can hear him swing his heavy sledge,
    With measured beat and slow,
Like a sexton ringing the village bell,
    When the evening sun is low.

And children coming home from school
    Look in at the open door;
They love to see the flaming forge,
    And hear the bellows roar,
And catch the burning sparks that fly
    Like chaff from a threshing floor.

He goes on Sunday to the church,
    And sits among his boys;
He hears the parson pray and preach,
    He hears his daughter's voice,
Singing in the village choir,
    And it makes his heart rejoice.

It sounds to him like her mother's voice,
    Singing in Paradise!

He needs must think of her once more,
    How in the grave she lies;
And with his hard, rough hand he wipes
    A tear out of his eyes.

Toiling, – rejoicing, – sorrowing,
    Onward through life he goes;
Each morning sees some task begin,
    Each evening sees it close;
Something attempted, something done,
    Has earned a night's repose.

Thanks, thanks to thee, my worthy friend,
    For the lesson thou hast taught!
Thus at the flaming forge of life
    Our fortunes must be wrought;
Thus on its sounding anvil shaped
    Each burning deed and thought!

The Rainy Day

The day is cold, and dark, and dreary;
It rains, and the wind is never weary;
The vine still clings to the mouldering wall,
But at every gust the dead leaves fall,
    And the day is dark and dreary.

My life is cold, and dark, and dreary;
It rains, and the wind is never weary;
My thoughts still cling to the mouldering Past,
But the hopes of youth fall thick in the blast,
    And the days are dark and dreary.

Be still, sad heart! and cease repining;
Behind the clouds is the sun still shining;
Thy fate is the common fate of all,
Into each life some rain must fall,
    Some days must be dark and dreary.

The Arsenal at Springfield

This is the Arsenal. From floor to ceiling,
    Like a huge organ, rise the burnished arms;
But from their silent pipes no anthem pealing
    Startles the villages with strange alarms.

Ah! what a sound will rise, how wild and dreary,
    When the death-angel touches those swift keys!
What loud lament and dismal Miserere
    Will mingle with their awful symphonies!

I hear even now the infinite fierce chorus,
    The cries of agony, the endless groan,
Which, through the ages that have gone before us,
    In long reverberations reach our own.

On helm and harness rings the Saxon hammer,
    Through Cimbric forest roars the Norseman's song,
And loud, amid the universal clamour,
    O'er distant deserts sounds the Tartar gong.

I hear the Florentine, who from his palace
    Wheels out his battle-bell with dreadful din,
And Aztec priests upon their teocallis
    Beat the wild war-drums made of serpent's skin;

The tumult of each sacked and burning village;
    The shout that every prayer for mercy drowns;
The soldiers' revels in the midst of pillage;
    The wail of famine in beleaguered towns;

The bursting shell, the gateway wrenched asunder,
    The rattling musketry, the clashing blade;
And ever and anon, in tones of thunder,
    The diapason of the cannonade.

Is it, O man, with such discordant noises,
    With such accursed instruments as these,

Thou drownest Nature's sweet and kindly voices,
    And jarrest the celestial harmonies?

Were half the power, that fills the world with terror,
    Were half the wealth, bestowed on camps and courts,
Given to redeem the human mind from error,
    There were no need of arsenals nor forts:

The warrior's name would be a name abhorred!
    And every nation, that should lift again
Its hand against a brother, on its forehead
    Would wear for evermore the curse of Cain!

Down the dark future, through long generations,
    The echoing sounds grow fainter and then cease;
And like a bell, with solemn, sweet vibrations,
    I hear once more the voice of Christ say, 'Peace!'

Peace! and no longer from its brazen portals
    The blast of War's great organ shakes the skies!
But beautiful as songs of the immortals,
    The holy melodies of love arise.

The Bridge

I stood on the bridge at midnight,
  As the clocks were striking the hour,
And the moon rose o'er the city,
  Behind the dark church-tower.

I saw her bright reflection
  In the waters under me,
Like a golden goblet falling
  And sinking into the sea.

And far in the hazy distance
  Of that lovely night in June,
The blaze of the flaming furnace
  Gleamed redder than the moon.

Among the long, black rafters
  The waving shadows lay,
And the current that came from the ocean
  Seemed to lift and bear them away;

As, sweeping and eddying through them,
  Rose the belated tide,
And, streaming into the moonlight,
  The seaweed floated wide.

And like those waters rushing
  Among the wooden piers,
A flood of thoughts came o'er me
  That filled my eyes with tears.

How often, O, how often,
  In the days that had gone by,
I had stood on that bridge at midnight,
  And gazed on that wave and sky!

How often, O, how often,
  I had wished that the ebbing tide

Would bear me away on its bosom
    O'er the ocean wild and wide!

For my heart was hot and restless,
    And my life was full of care,
And the burden laid upon me
    Seemed greater than I could bear.

But now it has fallen from me,
    It is buried in the sea;
And only the sorrow of others
    Throws its shadow over me.

Yet whenever I cross the river
    On its bridge with wooden piers,
Like the odour of brine from the ocean
    Comes the thought of other years.

And I think how many thousands
    Of care-encumbered men,
Each bearing his burden of sorrow,
    Have crossed the bridge since then.

I see the long procession
    Still passing to and fro,
The young heart hot and restless,
    And the old subdued and slow!

And for ever and for ever,
    As long as the river flows,
As long as the heart has passions,
    As long as life has woes;

The moon and its broken reflection
    And its shadows shall appear,
As the symbol of love in heaven,
    And its waving image here.

The Day is Done

The day is done, and the darkness
    Falls from the wings of Night,
As a feather is wafted downward
    From an eagle in his flight.

I see the lights of the village
    Gleam through the rain and the mist,
And a feeling of sadness comes o'er me,
    That my soul cannot resist:

A feeling of sadness and longing,
    That is not akin to pain,
And resembles sorrow only
    As the mist resembles the rain.

Come, read to me some poem,
    Some simple and heartfelt lay,
That shall soothe this restless feeling,
    And banish the thoughts of day.

Not from the grand old masters,
    Not from the bards sublime,
Whose distant footsteps echo
    Through the corridors of Time.

For, like strains of martial music,
    Their mighty thoughts suggest
Life's endless toil and endeavour;
    And to-night I long for rest.

Read from some humbler poet,
    Whose songs gushed from his heart,
As showers from the clouds of summer,
    Or tears from the eyelids start;

Who, through long days of labour,
    And nights devoid of ease,

Still heard in his soul the music
   Of wonderful melodies.

Such songs have power to quiet
   The restless pulse of care,
And come like the benediction
   That follows after prayer.

Then read from the treasured volume
   The poem of thy choice,
And lend to the rhyme of the poet
   The beauty of thy voice.

And the night shall be filled with music,
   And the cares that infest the day,
Shall fold their tents, like the Arabs,
   And as silently, steal away.

Afternoon in February

The day is ending,
The night is descending;
The marsh is frozen,
   The river dead.

Through clouds like ashes
The red sun flashes
On village windows
   That glimmer red.

The snow recommences;
The buried fences
Mark no longer
   The road o'er the plain;

While through the meadows,
Like fearful shadows,
Slowly passes
   A funeral train.

The bell is pealing,
And every feeling
Within me responds
   To the dismal knell;

Shadows are trailing,
My heart is bewailing
And toiling within
   Like a funeral bell.

The Arrow and the Song

I shot an arrow into the air,
It fell to earth, I knew not where;
For, so swiftly it flew, the sight
Could not follow it in its flight.

I breathed a song into the air,
It fell to earth, I knew not where;
For who has sight so keen and strong,
That it can follow the flight of song?

Long, long afterward, in an oak
I found the arrow, still unbroke;
And the song, from beginning to end,
I found again in the heart of a friend.

The Building of the Ship

'Build me straight, O worthy Master!
  Staunch and strong, a goodly vessel,
That shall laugh at all disaster,
  And with wave and whirlwind wrestle!'

The merchant's word
Delighted the Master heard;
For his heart was in his work, and the heart
Giveth grace unto every Art.
A quiet smile played round his lips,
As the eddies and dimples of the tide
Play round the bows of ships,
That steadily at anchor ride.
And with a voice that was full of glee,
He answered, 'Ere long we will launch
A vessel as goodly, and strong, and staunch,
As ever weathered a wintry sea!'

And first with nicest skill and art,
Perfect and finished in every part,
A little model the Master wrought,
Which should be to the larger plan
What the child is to the man,
Its counterpart in miniature;
That with a hand more swift and sure
The greater labour might be brought
To answer to his inward thought.
And as he laboured, his mind ran o'er
The various ships that were built of yore,
And above them all, and strangest of all
Towered the Great Harry, crank and tall,
Whose picture was hanging on the wall,
With bows and stern raised high in air,
And balconies hanging here and there,
And signal lanterns and flags afloat,
And eight round towers, like those that frown

From some old castle, looking down
Upon the drawbridge and the moat.
And he said with a smile, 'Our ship, I wis,
Shall be of another form than this!'

It was of another form, indeed;
Built for freight, and yet for speed,
A beautiful and gallant craft;
Broad in the beam, that the stress of the blast
Pressing down upon sail and mast,
Might not the sharp bows overwhelm;
Broad in the beam, but sloping aft
With graceful curve and slow degrees,
That she might be docile to the helm
And that the currents of parted seas,
Closing behind, with mighty force,
Might aid and not impede her course.

In the shipyard stood the Master,
    With the model of the vessel,
That should laugh at all disaster,
    And with wave and whirlwind wrestle!

Covering many a rood of ground,
Lay the timber piled around;
Timber of chestnut and elm and oak,
And scattered here and there, with these,
The knarred and crooked cedar knees;
Brought from regions far away,
From Pascagoula's sunny bay,
And the banks of the roaring Roanoke!
Oh! what a wondrous thing it is
To note how many wheels of toil
One thought, one word, can set in motion!
There's not a ship that sails the ocean,
But every climate, every soil,
Must bring its tribute, great or small,
And help to build the wooden wall!

The sun was rising o'er the sea,
And long the level shadows lay,

As if they, too, the beams would be
Of some great, airy argosy,
Framed and launched in a single day.
That silent architect, the sun,
Had hewn and laid them every one,
Ere the work of man was yet begun.
Beside the Master, when he spoke,
A youth, against an anchor leaning
Listened, to catch his slightest meaning.
Only the long waves, as they broke
In ripples on the pebbly beach,
Interrupted the old man's speech.
Beautiful they were, in sooth,
The old man and the fiery youth!
The old man, in whose busy brain
Many a ship that sailed the main
Was modelled o'er and o'er again; –
The fiery youth, who was to be
The heir of his dexterity,
The heir of his house, and his daughter's hand,
When he had built and launched from land
What the elder head had planned.

'Thus,' said he, 'will we build this ship!
Lay square the blocks upon the slip,
And follow well this plan of mine.
Choose the timbers with greatest care;
Of all that is unsound beware;
For only what is sound and strong
To this vessel shall belong.
Cedar of Maine and Georgia pine
Here together shall combine.
A goodly frame, and a goodly fame,
And the UNION be her name!
For the day that gives her to the sea
Shall give my daughter unto thee!'
The Master's word
Enraptured the young man heard;
And as he turned his face aside,

With a look of joy and a thrill of pride
Standing before
Her father's door,
He saw the form of his promised bride.

The sun shone on her golden hair,
And her cheek was glowing fresh and fair,
With the breath of morn and the soft sea air.
Like a beauteous barge was she,
Still at rest on the sandy beach,
Just beyond the billow's reach;
But he
Was the restless, seething, stormy sea!

Ah, how skilful grows the hand
That obeyeth Love's command!
It is the heart and not the brain,
That to the highest doth attain,
And he who followeth Love's behest
Far exceedeth all the rest!
Thus with the rising of the sun
Was the noble task begun,
And soon throughout the shipyard's bounds
Were heard the intermingled sounds
Of axes and of mallets, plied
With vigorous arms on every side;
Plied so deftly and so well,
That, ere the shadows of evening fell,
The keel of oak for a noble ship,
Scarfed and bolted, straight and strong,
Was lying ready, and stretched along
The blocks, well placed upon the slip.
Happy, thrice happy, every one
Who sees his labour well begun,
And not perplexed and multiplied,
By idly waiting for time and tide!

And when the hot, long day was o'er,
The young man at the Master's door
Sat with the maiden calm and still.

And within the porch, a little more
Removed beyond the evening chill,
The father sat, and told them tales
Of wrecks in the great September gales,
Of pirates upon the Spanish Main,
And ships that never came back again,
The chance and change of a sailor's life,
Want and plenty, rest and strife,
His roving fancy, like the wind,
That nothing can stay and nothing can bind,
And the magic charm of foreign lands,
With shadows of palms, and shining sands,
Where the tumbling surf,
O'er the coral reefs of Madagascar,
Washes the feet of the swarthy Lascar,
As he lies alone and asleep on the turf.
And the trembling maiden held her breath
At the tales of that awful, pitiless sea,
With all its terror and mystery,
The dim, dark sea, so like unto Death,
That divides and yet unites mankind!
And whenever the old man paused, a gleam
From the bowl of his pipe would awhile illume
The silent group in the twilight gloom,
And thoughtful faces, as in a dream;
And for a moment one might mark
What had been hidden by the dark,
That the head of the maiden lay at rest,
Tenderly, on the young man's breast!

Day by day the vessel grew,
With timbers fashioned strong and true,
Stemson and keelson and sternson-knee,
Till, framed with perfect symmetry,
A skeleton ship rose up to view!
All around the bows and along the side
The heavy hammers and mallets plied,
Till, after many a week, at length,
Wonderful for form and strength,
Sublime in its enormous bulk,

Loomed aloft the shadowy hulk!
And around it columns of smoke, upwreathing,
Rose from the boiling, bubbling, seething
Caldron, that glowed,
And overflowed
With the black tar, heated for the sheathing.
And amid the clamours
Of clattering hammers,
He who listened heard now and then
The song of the Master and his men: –

'Build me straight, O worthy Master,
    Staunch and strong, a goodly vessel,
That shall laugh at all disaster,
    And with wave and whirlwind wrestle!'

With oaken brace and copper band,
Lay the rudder on the sand,
That, like a thought, should have control
Over the movement of the whole;
And near it the anchor, whose giant hand
Would reach down and grapple with the land,
And immovable and fast
Hold the great ship against the bellowing blast!
And at the bows an image stood,
By a cunning artist carved in wood,
With robes of white, that far behind
Seemed to be fluttering in the wind.
It was not shaped in a classic mould,
Not like a Nymph or Goddess of old,
Or Naiad rising from the water,
But modelled from the Master's daughter!
On many a dreary and misty night,
'Twill be seen by the rays of the signal light,
Speeding along through the rain and the dark,
Like a ghost in its snow-white sark,
The pilot of some phantom bark,
Guiding the vessel, in its flight,
By a path none other knows aright!
Behold, at last

Each tall and tapering mast
Is swung into its place;
Shrouds and stays
Holding it firm and fast!

Long ago,
In the deer-haunted forests of Maine,
When upon mountain and plain
Lay the snow,
They fell, – those lordly pines!
Those grand, majestic pines!
Mid shouts and cheers
The jaded steers,
Panting beneath the goad,
Dragged down the weary, winding road
Those captive kings so straight and tall.
To be shorn of their streaming hair,
And, naked and bare,
To feel the stress and the strain
Of the wind and the reeling main,
Whose roar
Would remind them for evermore
Of their native forests they should not see again.

And everywhere
The slender, graceful spars
Poise aloft in the air,
And at the mast-head,
White, blue, and red,
A flag unrolls the stripes and stars.
Ah! when the wanderer, lonely, friendless,
In foreign harbours shall behold
That flag unrolled,
'Twill be as a friendly hand
Stretched out from his native land,
Filling his heart with memories sweet and endless!

All is finished! and at length
Has come the bridal day
Of beauty and of strength.

To-day the vessel shall be launched!
With fleecy clouds the sky is blanched,
And o'er the bay,
Slowly, in all his splendours dight,
The great sun rises to behold the sight.

The ocean old,
Centuries old,
Strong as youth, and as uncontrolled,
Paces restless to and fro,
Up and down the sands of gold.
His beating heart is not at rest;
And far and wide,
With ceaseless flow,
His beard of snow
Heaves with the heaving of his breast.
He waits impatient for his bride.
There she stands,
With her foot upon the sands,
Decked with flags and streamers gay,
In honour of her marriage day,
Her snow-white signals fluttering, blending,
Round her like a veil descending,
Ready to be
The bride of the gray, old sea.

On the deck another bride
Is standing by her lover's side.
Shadows from the flags and shrouds,
Like the shadows cast by clouds,
Broken by many a sunny fleck,
Fall around them on the deck.

The prayer is said,
The service read,
The joyous bridegroom bows his head.
And in tears the good old Master
Shakes the brown hand of his son,
Kisses his daughter's glowing cheek
In silence, for he cannot speak,

And ever faster
Down his own the tears begin to run.
The worthy pastor –
The shepherd of that wandering flock,
That has the ocean for its wold,
That has the vessel for its fold,
Leaping ever from rock to rock –
Spake, with accents mild and clear,
Words of warning, words of cheer,
But tedious to the bridegroom's ear.

He knew the chart
Of the sailor's heart,
All its pleasures and its griefs,
All its shallows and rocky reefs,
All those secret currents, that flow
With such resistless undertow,
And lift and drift, with terrible force,
The will from its moorings and its course,
Therefore he spake, and thus said he: –
'Like unto ships far off at sea,
Outward or homeward bound, are we.
Before, behind and all around,
Floats and swings the horizon's bound,
Seems at its distant rim to rise
And climb the crystal wall of the skies,
And then again to turn and sink,
As if we could slide from its outer brink.
Ah! it is not the sea,
It is not the sea that sinks and shelves,
But ourselves
That rock and rise
With endless and uneasy motion,
Now touching the very skies,
Now sinking into the depths of ocean.
Ah! if our souls but poise and swing
Like the compass in its brazen ring,
Ever level and ever true
To the toil and the task we have to do,
We shall sail securely, and safely reach

The Fortunate Isles, on whose shining beach
The sights we see, and the sounds we hear,
Will be those of joy and not of fear!'

Then the Master,
With a gesture of command,
Waved his hand;
And at the word,
Loud and sudden there was heard,
All around them and below,
The sound of hammers, blow on blow,
Knocking away the shores and spurs.
And see! she stirs!
She starts, – she moves, – she seems to feel
The thrill of life along her keel,
And, spurning with her foot the ground,
With one exulting, joyous, bound,
She leaps into the ocean's arms!
And lo! from the assembled crowd
There rose a shout, prolonged and loud,
That to the ocean seemed to say, –
'Take her, O bridegroom, old and gray,
Take her to thy protecting arms,
With all her youth and all her charms!'
How beautiful she is! How fair
She lies within those arms, that press
Her form with many a soft caress
Of tenderness and watchful care!
Sail forth into the sea, O ship!
Through wind and wave, right onward steer!
The moistened eye, the trembling lip,
Are not the signs of doubt or fear.
Sail forth into the sea of life,
O gentle, loving, trusting wife,
And safe from all adversity
Upon the bosom of that sea
Thy comings and thy goings be!
For gentleness and love and trust
Prevail o'er angry wave and gust;

And in the wreck of noble lives
Something immortal still survives!

Thou, too, sail on, O Ship of State!
Sail on, O UNION, strong and great!
Humanity with all its fears,
With all the hopes of future years,
Is hanging breathless on thy fate!
We know what Master laid thy keel,
What Workmen wrought thy ribs of steel,
Who made each mast, and sail, and rope,
What anvils rang, what hammers beat,
In what a forge and what a heat
Were shaped the anchors of thy hope!
Fear not each sudden sound and shock,
'Tis of the wave and not the rock;
'Tis but the flapping of the sail,
And not a rent made by the gale!
In spite of rock and tempest's roar,
In spite of false lights on the shore,
Sail on, nor fear to breast the sea!
Our hearts, our hopes, are all with thee,
Our hearts, our hopes, our prayers, our tears,
Our faith triumphant o'er our fears,
Are all with thee, – are all with thee!

The Fire of Drift-Wood

We sat within the farmhouse old,
   Whose windows, looking o'er the bay,
Gave to the sea-breeze, damp and cold,
   An easy entrance, night and day.

Not far away we saw the port, –
   The strange, old-fashioned, silent town, –
The lighthouse, – the dismantled fort, –
   The wooden houses, quaint and brown.

We sat and talked until the night,
   Descending, filled the little room;
Our faces faded from the sight,
   Our voices only broke the gloom.

We spake of many a vanished scene,
   Of what we once had thought and said,
Of what had been, and might have been,
   And who was changed, and who was dead.

And all that fills the hearts of friends,
   When first they feel, with secret pain,
Their lives thenceforth have separate ends,
   And never can be one again;

The first slight swerving of the heart,
   That words are powerless to express,
And leave it still unsaid in part,
   Or say it in too great excess.

The very tones in which we spake
   Had something strange, I could but mark;
The leaves of memory seemed to make
   A mournful rustling in the dark.

Oft died the words upon our lips,
   As suddenly, from out the fire

Built of the wreck of stranded ships,
  The flames would leap and then expire.

And, as their splendour flashed and failed,
  We thought of wrecks upon the main, –
Of ships dismasted, that were hailed
  And sent no answer back again.

The windows, rattling in their frames, –
  The ocean, roaring up the beach, –
The gusty blast, – the bickering flames,
  All mingled vaguely in our speech;

Until they made themselves a part
  Of fancies floating through the brain,
The long-lost ventures of the heart,
  That send no answers back again.

O flames that glowed! O hearts that yearned!
  They were indeed too much akin,
The drift-wood fire without that burned,
  The thoughts that burned and glowed within.

The Builders

All are architects of Fate,
  Working in these walls of Time;
Some with massive deeds and great,
  Some with ornaments of rhyme.

Nothing useless is, or low;
  Each thing in its place is best;
And what seems but idle show
  Strengthens and supports the rest.

For the structure that we raise,
  Time is with materials filled;
Our to-days and yesterdays
  Are the blocks with which we build.

Truly shape and fashion these;
  Leave no yawning gaps between;
Think not, because no man sees,
  Such things will remain unseen.

In the elder days of Art,
  Builders wrought with greatest care
Each minute an unseen part;
  For the Gods see everywhere.

Let us do our work as well,
  Both the unseen and the seen!
Make the house, where Gods may dwell,
  Beautiful, entire, and clean.

Else our lives are incomplete,
  Standing in these walls of Time,
Broken stairways, where the feet
  Stumble as they seek to climb.

Build to-day, then, strong and sure,
  With a firm and ample base;

And ascending and secure
  Shall to-morrow find its place.

Thus alone can we attain
  To those turrets, where the eye
Sees the world as one vast plain,
  And one boundless reach of sky.

The Ladder of St Augustine

Saint Augustine! well hast thou said,
   That of our vices we can frame
A ladder, if we will but tread
   Beneath our feet each deed of shame!

All common things, each day's events,
   That with the hour begin and end,
Our pleasures and our discontents,
   Are rounds by which we may ascend.

The low desire, the base design,
   That makes another's virtues less;
The revel of the ruddy wine,
   And all occasions of excess;

The longing for ignoble things;
   The strife for triumph more than truth;
The hardening of the heart, that brings
   Irreverence for the dreams of youth;

All thoughts of ill; all evil deeds,
   That have their root in thoughts of ill;
Whatever hinders or impedes
   The action of the nobler will; –

All these must first be trampled down
   Beneath our feet, if we would gain
In the bright fields of fair renown
   The right of eminent domain.

We have not wings, we cannot soar;
   But we have feet to scale and climb
By slow degrees, by more and more,
   The cloudy summits of our time.

The mighty pyramids of stone
   That wedge-like cleave the desert airs,

When nearer seen, and better known,
   Are but gigantic flights of stairs.

The distant mountains, that uprear
   Their solid bastions to the skies,
Are crossed by pathways, that appear
   As we to higher levels rise.

The heights by great men reached and kept
   Were not attained by sudden flight,
But they, while their companions slept,
   Were toiling upward in the night.

Standing on what too long we bore
   With shoulders bent and downcast eyes,
We may discern – unseen before –
   A path to higher destinies.

Nor deem the irrevocable Past,
   As wholly wasted, wholly vain,
If, rising on its wrecks, at last
   To something nobler we attain.

Haunted Houses

All houses wherein men have lived and died
    Are haunted houses. Through the open doors
The harmless phantoms on their errands glide,
    With feet that make no sound upon the floors.

We meet them at the door-way, on the stair,
    Along the passages they come and go,
Impalpable impressions on the air,
    A sense of something moving to and fro.

There are more guests at table, than the hosts
    Invited; the illuminated hall
Is thronged with quiet, inoffensive ghosts,
    As silent as the pictures on the wall.

The stranger at my fireside cannot see
    The forms I see, nor hear the sounds I hear;
He but perceives what is; while unto me
    All that has been is visible and clear.

We have no title-deeds to house or lands;
    Owners and occupants of earlier dates
From graves forgotten stretch their dusty hands,
    And hold in mortmain still their old estates.

The spirit-world around this world of sense
    Floats like an atmosphere, and everywhere
Wafts through these earthly mists and vapours dense
    A vital breath of more ethereal air.

Our little lives are kept in equipoise
    By opposite attractions and desires;
The struggle of the instinct that enjoys,
    And the more noble instinct that aspires.

These perturbations, this perpetual jar
    Of earthly wants and aspirations high,

Come from the influence of an unseen star,
   An undiscovered planet in our sky.

And as the moon from some dark gate of cloud
   Throws o'er the sea a floating bridge of light,
Across whose trembling planks our fancies crowd,
   Into the realm of mystery and night, –

So from the world of spirits there descends
   A bridge of light, connecting it with this,
O'er whose unsteady floor, that sways and bends,
   Wander our thoughts above the dark abyss.

In the Churchyard at Cambridge

In the village churchyard she lies,
Dust is in her beautiful eyes,
    No more she breathes, nor feels, nor stirs;
At her feet and at her head
Lies a slave to attend the dead,
    But their dust is white as hers.

Was she a lady of high degree,
So much in love with the vanity
    And foolish pomp of this world of ours?
Or was it Christian charity,
And lowliness and humility,
    The richest and rarest of all dowers?

Who shall tell us? No one speaks;
No colour shoots into those cheeks,
    Either of anger or of pride,
At the rude question we have asked;
Nor will the mystery be unmasked
    By those who are sleeping at her side.

Hereafter? – And do you think to look
On the terrible pages of that Book
    To find her failings, faults, and errors?
Ah, you will then have other cares,
In your own shortcomings and despairs,
    In your own secret sins and terrors!

The Two Angels

Two angels, one of Life and one of Death,
   Passed o'er our village as the morning broke;
The dawn was on their faces, and beneath,
   The sombre houses hearsed with plumes of smoke.

Their attitude and aspect were the same,
   Alike their features and their robes of white;
But one was crowned with amaranth, as with flame,
   And one with asphodels, like flakes of light.

I saw them pause on their celestial way;
   Then said I, with deep fear and doubt oppressed,
'Beat not so loud, my heart, lest thou betray
   The place where thy beloved are at rest!'

And he who wore the crown of asphodels,
   Descending, at my door began to knock,
And my soul sank within me, as in wells
   The waters sink before an earthquake's shock.

I recognised the nameless agony,
   The terror and the tremor and the pain,
That oft before had filled or haunted me,
   And now returned with threefold strength again.

The door I opened to my heavenly guest,
   And listened, for I thought I heard God's voice;
And, knowing whatsoe'er he sent was best,
   Dared neither to lament nor to rejoice.

Then with a smile, that filled the house with light,
   'My errand is not Death, but Life,' he said;
And ere I answered, passing out of sight,
   On his celestial embassy he sped.

'Twas at thy door, O friend! and not at mine,
   The angel with the amaranthine wreath,

Pausing, descended, and with voice divine,
    Whispered a word that had a sound like Death.

Then fell upon the house a sudden gloom,
    A shadow on those features fair and thin;
And softly, from that hushed and darkened room,
    Two angels issued, where but one went in.

All is of God! If he but wave his hand,
    The mists collect, the rain falls thick and loud,
Till, with a smile of light on sea and land,
    Lo! he looks back from the departing cloud.

Angels of Life and Death alike are his;
    Without his leave they pass no threshold o'er;
Who, then, would wish or dare, believing this,
    Against his messengers to shut the door?

The Jewish Cemetery at Newport

How strange it seems! These Hebrews in their graves,
 Close by the street of this fair seaport town.
Silent beside the never-silent waves,
 At rest in all this moving up and down!

The trees are white with dust, that o'er their sleep
 Wave their broad curtains in the south-wind's breath,
While underneath such leafy tents they keep
 The long, mysterious Exodus of Death.

And these sepulchral stones, so old and brown,
 That pave with level flags their burial-place,
Seem like the tablets of the Law, thrown down
 And broken by Moses at the mountain's base.

The very names recorded here are strange,
 Of foreign accent, and of different climes:
Alvares and Rivera interchange
 With Abraham and Jacob of old times.

'Blessed be God! for he created Death!'
 The mourners said, 'and Death is rest and peace';
Then added, in the certainty of faith,
 'And giveth Life that never more shall cease.'

Closed are the portals of their Synagogue,
 No Psalms of David now the silence break,
No Rabbi reads the ancient Decalogue
 In the grand dialect the Prophets spake.

Gone are the living, but the dead remain,
 And not neglected; for a hand unseen,
Scattering its bounty, like a summer rain,
 Still keeps their graves and their remembrance green.

How came they here? What burst of Christian hate,
 What persecution, merciless and blind,

Drove o'er the sea – that desert desolate –
   These Ishmaels and Hagars of mankind?

They lived in narrow streets and lanes obscure,
   Ghetto and Judenstrass, in mirk and mire;
Taught in the school of patience to endure
   The life of anguish and the death of fire.

All their lives long, with the unleavened bread
   And bitter herbs of exile and its fears,
The wasting famine of the heart they fed,
   And slaked its thirst with marah of their tears.

Anathema maranatha! was the cry
   That rang from town to town, from street to street;
At every gate the accursed Mordecai
   Was mocked and jeered, and spurned by Christian feet.

Pride and humiliation hand in hand
   Walked with them through the world where'er they went;
Trampled and beaten were they as the sand,
   And yet unshaken as the continent.

For in the background figures vague and vast
   Of patriarchs and prophets rose sublime,
And all the great traditions of the Past
   They saw reflected in the coming time.

And thus for ever with reverted look
   The mystic volume of the world they read,
Spelling it backward, like a Hebrew book.
   Till life became a Legend of the Dead.

But ah! what once has been shall be no more!
   The groaning earth in travail and in pain
Brings forth its races, but does not restore,
   And the dead nations never rise again.

My Lost Youth

Often I think of the beautiful town
   That is seated by the sea;
Often in thought go up and down
The pleasant streets of that dear old town.
     And my youth comes back to me,
       And a verse of a Lapland song
       Is haunting my memory still:
     'A boy's will is the wind's will,
And the thoughts of youth are long, long thoughts.'

I can see the shadowy lines of its trees,
   And catch, in sudden gleams,
The sheen of the far-surrounding seas,
And islands that were the Hesperides
     Of all my boyish dreams.
       And the burden of that old song,
       It murmurs and whispers still:
     'A boy's will is the wind's will,
And the thoughts of youth are long, long thoughts.'

I remember the black wharves and the slips,
   And the sea-tides tossing free;
And Spanish sailors with bearded lips,
And the beauty and mystery of the ships,
     And the magic of the sea.
       And the voice of that wayward song,
       Is singing and saying still:
     'A boy's will is the wind's will,
And the thoughts of youth are long, long thoughts.'

I remember the bulwarks by the shore,
   And the fort upon the hill;
The sunrise gun, with its hollow roar,
The drum-beat repeated o'er and o'er,
     And the bugle wild and shrill.
       And the music of that old song

Throbs in my memory still:
'A boy's will is the wind's will,
And the thoughts of youth are long, long thoughts.'

I remember the sea-fight far away,
How it thundered o'er the tide!
And the dead captains, as they lay
In their graves, o'erlooking the tranquil bay,
Where they in battle died.
And the sound of that mournful song
Goes through me with a thrill:
'A boy's will is the wind's will,
And the thoughts of youth are long, long thoughts.'

I can see the breezy dome of groves,
The shadows of Deering's Woods;
And the friendships old and the early loves
Come back with a Sabbath sound, as of doves
In quiet neighbourhoods.
And the verse of that sweet old song,
It flutters and murmurs still:
'A boy's will is the wind's will,
And the thoughts of youth are long, long thoughts.'

I remember the gleams and glooms that dart
Across the schoolboy's brain;
The song and the silence in the heart,
That in part are prophecies, and in part
Are longings wild and vain.
And the voice of that fitful song
Sings on, and is never still:
'A boy's will is the wind's will,
And the thoughts of youth are long, long thoughts.'

There are things of which I may not speak;
There are dreams that cannot die;
There are thoughts that make the strong heart weak,
And bring a pallor into the cheek,
And a mist before the eye.
And the words to that fatal song

Come over me like a chill:
  'A boy's will is the wind's will,
And the thoughts of youth are long, long thoughts.'

Strange to me now are the forms I meet
  When I visit the dear old town;
But the native air is pure and sweet,
And the trees that o'ershadow each well-known street,
  As they balance up and down,
    Are singing the beautiful song,
    Are sighing and whispering still:
  'A boy's will is the wind's will,
And the thoughts of youth are long, long thoughts.'

And Deering's Woods are fresh and fair,
  And with joy that is almost pain
My heart goes back to wander there,
And among the dreams of the days that were,
  I find my lost youth again.
    And the strange and beautiful song,
    The groves are repeating it still:
  'A boy's will is the wind's will,
And the thoughts of youth are long, long thoughts.'

The Ropewalk

In that building, long and low,
With its windows all a-row,
    Like the port-holes of a hulk,
Human spiders spin and spin,
Backward down their threads so thin
    Dropping, each a hempen bulk.

At the end, an open door;
Squares of sunshine on the floor
    Light the long and dusky lane;
And the whirring of a wheel,
Dull and drowsy, makes me feel
    All its spokes are in my brain.

As the spinners to the end
Downward go and reascend,
    Gleam the long threads in the sun;
While within this brain of mine
Cobwebs brighter and more fine
    By the busy wheel are spun.

Two fair maidens in a swing,
Like white doves upon the wing,
    First before my vision pass;
Laughing, as their gentle hands
Closely clasp the twisted strands,
    At their shadow on the grass.

Then a booth of mountebanks,
With its smell of tan and planks,
    And a girl poised high in air
On a cord, in spangled dress,
With a faded loveliness,
    And a weary look of care.

Then a homestead among farms,
And a woman with bare arms

Drawing water from a well;
As the bucket mounts apace,
With it mounts her own fair face,
   As at some magician's spell.

Then an old man in a tower,
Ringing loud the noontide hour,
   While the rope coils round and round
Like a serpent at his feet,
And again, in swift retreat,
   Nearly lifts him from the ground.

Then within a prison-yard,
Faces fixed, and stern, and hard,
   Laughter and indecent mirth;
Ah! it is the gallows-tree!
Breath of Christian charity,
   Blow, and sweep it from the earth!

Then a schoolboy, with his kite
Gleaming in a sky of light,
   And an eager, upward look;
Steeds pursued through land and field;
Fowlers with their snares concealed;
   And an angler by a brook.

Ships rejoicing in the breeze,
Wrecks that float o'er unknown seas,
   Anchors dragged through faithless sand;
Sea-fog drifting overhead,
And, with lessening line and lead,
   Sailors feeling for the land.

All these scenes do I behold,
These, and many left untold,
   In that building long and low;
While the wheel goes round and round,
With a drowsy, dreamy sound,
   And the spinners backward go.

Something Left Undone

Labour with what zeal we will,
   Something still remains undone,
Something uncompleted still
   Waits the rising of the sun.

By the bedside, on the stair,
   At the threshold, near the gates,
With its menace or its prayer,
   Like a mendicant it waits;

Waits, and will not go away;
   Waits, and will not be gainsaid;
By the cares of yesterday
   Each to-day is heavier made;

Till at length the burden seems
   Greater than our strength can bear,
Heavy as the weight of dreams,
   Pressing on us everywhere.

And we stand from day to day,
   Like the dwarfs of times gone by,
Who, as Northern legends say,
   On their shoulders held the sky.

The Haunted Chamber

Each heart has its haunted chamber,
    Where the silent moonlight falls!
On the floor are mysterious footsteps,
    There are whispers along the walls!

And mine at times is haunted
    By phantoms of the Past,
As motionless as shadows
    By the silent moonlight cast.

A form sits by the window,
    That is not seen by day,
For as soon as the dawn approaches
    It vanishes away.

It sits there in the moonlight,
    Itself as pale and still,
And points with its airy finger
    Across the window-sill.

Without, before the window,
    There stands a gloomy pine,
Whose boughs wave upward and downward
    As wave these thoughts of mine.

And underneath its branches
    Is the grave of a little child,
Who died upon life's threshold,
    And never wept nor smiled.

What are ye, O pallid phantoms!
    That haunt my troubled brain?
That vanish when day approaches,
    And at night return again?

What are ye, O pallid phantoms!
　But the statues without breath,
That stand on the bridge overarching
　The silent river of death?

Vox Populi

When Mazárvan the magician
   Journeyed westward through Cathay,
Nothing heard he but the praises
   Of Badoura on his way.

But the lessening rumour ended
   When he came to Khaledan,
There the folk were talking only
   Of Prince Camaralzaman.

So it happens with the poets:
   Every province hath its own;
Camaralzaman is famous
   Where Badoura is unknown.

Changed

From the outskirts of the town,
  Where of old the mile-stone stood,
Now a stranger, looking down
I behold the shadowy crown
  Of the dark and haunted wood.

Is it changed, or am I changed?
  Ah! the oaks are fresh and green,
But the friends with whom I ranged
Through their thickets are estranged
  By the years that intervene.

Bright as ever flows the sea,
  Bright as ever shines the sun,
But, alas! they seem to me
Not the sun that used to be,
  Not the tides that used to run.

Palingenesis

I lay upon the headland-height, and listened
To the incessant sobbing of the sea
   In caverns under me,
And watched the waves, that tossed and fled and glistened
Until the rolling meadows of amethyst
   Melted away in mist.

Then suddenly, as one from sleep, I started;
For round about me all the sunny capes
   Seemed peopled with the shapes
Of those whom I had known in days departed,
Apparelled in the loveliness which gleams
   On faces seen in dreams.

A moment only, and the light and glory
Faded away, and the disconsolate shore
   Stood lonely as before;
And the wild-roses of the promontory
Around me shuddered in the wind, and shed
   Their petals of pale red.

There was an old belief that in the embers
Of all things their primordial form exists,
   And cunning alchemists
Could re-create the rose with all its members
From its own ashes, but without the bloom,
   Without the lost perfume.

Ah me! What wonder-working, occult science
Can from the ashes in our hearts once more
   The rose of youth restore?
What craft of alchemy can bid defiance
To time and change, and for a single hour
   Renew this phantom-flower?

'Oh, give me back,' I cried, 'the vanished splendours,
The breath of morn, and the exultant strife,

When the swift stream of life
Bounds o'er its rocky channel, and surrenders
The pond, with all its lilies, for the leap
   Into the unknown deep!'

And the sea answered, with a lamentation,
Like some old prophet wailing, and it said,
   'Alas! thy youth is dead!
It breathes no more, its heart has no pulsation;
In the dark places with the dead of old
   It lies for ever cold!'

Then said I, 'From its consecrated cerements
I will not drag this sacred dust again,
   Only to give me pain;
But, still remembering all the lost endearments,
Go on my way, like one who looks before,
   And turns to weep no more.'

Into what land of harvests, what plantations
Bright with autumnal foliage and the glow
   Of sunsets burning low;
Beneath what midnight skies, whose constellations
Light up the spacious avenues between
   This world and the unseen!

Amid what friendly greetings and caresses,
What households, though not alien, yet not mine,
   What bowers of rest divine;
To what temptations in lone wildernesses,
What famine of the heart, what pain and loss,
   The bearing of what cross!

I do not know; nor will I vainly question
Those pages of the mystic book which hold
   The story still untold,
But without rash conjecture or suggestion
Turn its last leaves in reverence and good heed,
   Until 'The End' I read.

Concord

[Nathaniel Hawthorne]
May 23, 1864

How beautiful it was, that one bright day
   In the long week of rain!
Though all its splendour could not chase away
   The omnipresent pain.

The lovely town was white with apple-blooms,
   And the great elms o'erhead
Dark shadows wove on their ærial looms
   Shot through with golden thread.

Across the meadows, by the gray old manse,
   The historic river flowed; –
I was as one who wanders in a trance,
   Unconscious of his road.

The faces of familiar friends seemed strange;
   Their voices I could hear,
And yet the words they uttered seemed to change
   Their meaning to my ear.

For the one face I looked for was not there,
   The one low voice was mute;
Only an unseen presence filled the air,
   And baffled my pursuit.

Now I look back, and meadow, manse, and stream
   Dimly my thought defines;
I only see – a dream within a dream –
   The hill-top hearsed with pines.

I only hear above his place of rest
   Their tender undertone,
The infinite longings of a troubled breast,
   The voice so like his own.

There in seclusion and remote from men
    The wizard hand lies cold,
Which at its topmost speed let fall the pen,
    And left the tale half told.

Ah! who shall lift that wand of magic power,
    And the lost clue regain?
The unfinished window in Aladdin's tower
    Unfinished must remain!

To-morrow

'Tis late at night, and in the realm of sleep
   My little lambs are folded like the flocks;
   From room to room I hear the wakeful clocks
   Challenge the passing hour, like guards that keep
Their solitary watch on tower and steep;
   Far off I hear the crowing of the cocks,
   And through the opening door that time unlocks
   Feel the fresh breathing of To-morrow creep.
To-morrow! the mysterious, unknown guest,
   Who cries to me: 'Remember Barmecide,
   And tremble to be happy with the rest.'
And I make answer: 'I am satisfied;
   I dare not ask; I know not what is best;
   God hath already said what shall betide.'

On Translating the Divina Commedia

FIRST SONNET

Oft have I seen at some cathedral door
  A labourer, pausing in the dust and heat,
  Lay down his burden, and with reverent feet
  Enter, and cross himself, and on the floor
Kneel to repeat his paternoster o'er:
  Far off the noises of the world retreat;
  The loud vociferations of the street
  Become an undistinguishable roar.
So, as I enter here from day to day,
  And leave my burden at this minster-gate,
  Kneeling in prayer, and not ashamed to pray,
The tumult of the time disconsolate
  To inarticulate murmurs dies away,
While the eternal ages watch and wait.

SECOND SONNET

How strange the sculptures that adorn these towers;
  This crowd of statues, in whose folded sleeves
  Birds build their nests; while canopied with leaves
  Parvis and portal bloom like trellised bowers,
And the vast minster seems a cross of flowers!
  But fiends and dragons on the gargoyled eaves
  Watch the dead Christ between the living thieves,
  And, underneath, the traitor Judas lowers!
Ah! from what agonies of heart and brain
  What exultations trampling on despair,
  What tenderness, what tears, what hate of wrong,
What passionate outcry of a soul in pain,
  Uprose this poem of the earth and air,
  This mediæval miracle of song!

THIRD SONNET

I enter, and I see thee in the gloom
    Of the long aisles, O poet saturnine!
    And strive to make my steps keep pace with thine.
    The air is filled with some unknown perfume;
The congregation of the dead make room
    For thee to pass; the votive tapers shine;
    Like rooks that haunt Ravenna's groves of pine
    The hovering echoes fly from tomb to tomb.
From the confessionals I hear arise
    Rehearsals of forgotten tragedies
    And lamentations from the crypts below;
And then a voice celestial that begins
    With the pathetic words, 'Although your sins
    As scarlet be,' and ends with 'as the snow.'

FOURTH SONNET

With snow-white veil and garments as of flame,
    She stands before thee, who so long ago
    Filled thy young heart with passion and the woe
    From which thy song and all its splendours came;
And while with stern rebuke she speaks thy name,
    The ice about thy heart melts as the snow
    On mountain heights, and in swift overflow
    Comes gushing from thy lips in sobs of shame.
Thou makest full confession; and a gleam,
    As of the dawn on some dark forest cast,
    Seems on thy lifted forehead to increase;
Lethe and Eunoe – the remembered dream
    And the forgotten sorrow – bring at last
    That perfect pardon which is perfect peace.

FIFTH SONNET

I lift mine eyes, and all the windows blaze
    With forms of Saints and holy men who died,
    Here martyred and hereafter glorified;
    And the great Rose upon its leaves displays
Christ's Triumph, and the angelic roundelays,

With splendour upon splendour multiplied;
And Beatrice again at Dante's side
No more rebukes, but smiles her words of praise.
And then the organ sounds, and unseen choirs
Sing the old Latin hymns of peace and love
And benedictions of the Holy Ghost;
And the melodious bells among the spires
O'er all the house-tops and through heaven above
Proclaim the elevation of the Host!

SIXTH SONNET

O star of morning and of liberty!
O bringer of the light, whose splendour shines
Above the darkness of the Apennines,
Forerunner of the day that is to be!
The voices of the city and the sea,
The voices of the mountains and the pines,
Repeat thy song, till the familiar lines
Are footpaths for the thought of Italy!
Thy fame is blown abroad from all the heights,
Through all the nations, and a sound is heard,
As of a mighty wind, and men devout,
Strangers of Rome, and the new proselytes,
In their own language hear thy wondrous word,
And many are amazed and many doubt.

Nature

As a fond mother, when the day is o'er,
   Leads by the hand her little child to bed,
   Half willing, half reluctant to be led,
   And leave his broken playthings on the floor,
Still gazing at them through the open door,
   Nor wholly reassured and comforted
   By promises of others in their stead,
   Which, though more splendid, may not please him more;
So Nature deals with us, and takes away
   Our playthings one by one, and by the hand
   Leads us to rest so gently, that we go
Scarce knowing if we wished to go or stay,
   Being too full of sleep to understand
   How far the unknown transcends the what we know.

The Broken Oar

Once upon Iceland's solitary strand
   A poet wandered with his book and pen,
   Seeking some final word, some sweet Amen,
   Wherewith to close the volume in his hand.
The billows rolled and plunged upon the sand,
   The circling sea-gulls swept beyond his ken,
   And from the parting cloud-rack now and then
   Flashed the red sunset over sea and land.
Then by the billows at his feet was tossed
   A broken oar; and carved thereon he read,
   'Oft was I weary, when I toiled at thee';
And like a man, who findeth what was lost,
   He wrote the words, then lifted up his head,
   And flung his useless pen into the sea.

Kéramos

1878

Turn, turn, my wheel! Turn round and round
Without a pause, without a sound:
So spins the flying world away!
This clay, well mixed with marl and sand,
Follows the motion of my hand;
For some must follow, and some command,
Though all are made of clay!

Thus sang the Potter at his task
Beneath the blossoming hawthorn-tree,
While o'er his features, like a mask,
The quilted sunshine and leaf-shade
Moved, as the boughs above him swayed,
And clothed him, till he seemed to be
A figure woven in tapestry,
So sumptuously was he arrayed
In that magnificent attire
Of sable tissue flaked with fire.
Like a magician he appeared,
A conjurer without book or beard;
And while he plied his magic art –
For it was magical to me –
I stood in silence and apart,
And wondered more and more to see
That shapeless, lifeless mass of clay
Rise up to meet the master's hand,
And now contract, and now expand,
And even his slightest touch obey;
While ever in a thoughtful mood
He sang his ditty, and at times
Whistled a tune between the rhymes,
As a melodious interlude.

Turn, turn, my wheel! All things must change
To something new, to something strange;
Nothing that is can pause or stay;

The moon will wax, the moon will wane,
The mist and cloud will turn to rain,
The rain to mist and cloud again,
  To-morrow be to-day.

Thus still the Potter sang, and still,
By some unconscious act of will,
The melody and even the words
Were intermingled with my thought,
As bits of coloured thread are caught
And woven into nests of birds.
And thus to regions far remote,
Beyond the ocean's vast expanse,
This wizard in the motley coat
Transported me on wings of song,
And by the northern shores of France
Bore me with restless speed along.

What land is this that seems to be
A mingling of the land and sea?
This land of sluices, dikes, and dunes?
This water-net, that tessellates
The landscape? This unending maze
Of gardens, through whose latticed gates
The imprisoned pinks and tulips gaze;
Where in the long summer afternoons
The sunshine, softened by the haze,
Comes streaming down as through a screen;
Where over the fields and pastures green
The painted ships float high in air,
And over all and everywhere
The sails of windmills sink and soar
Like wings of sea-gulls on the shore?

What land is this? Yon pretty town
Is Delft, with all its wares displayed;
The pride, the market-place, the crown
And centre of the Potter's trade.
See! every house and room is bright
With glimmers of reflected light

From plates that on the dresser shine;
Flagons to foam with Flemish beer,
Or sparkle with the Rhenish wine,
And pilgrim flasks with fleur-de-lis,
And ships upon a rolling sea,
And tankards pewter topped, and queer
With comic mask and musketeer!
Each hospitable chimney smiles
A welcome from its painted tiles;
The parlour walls, the chamber floors,
The stairways and the corridors,
The borders of the garden walks,
Are beautiful with fadeless flowers,
That never droop in winds or showers,
And never wither on their stalks.

Turn, turn, my wheel! All life is brief;
What now is bud will soon be leaf,
   What now is leaf will soon decay;
The wind blows east, the wind blows west;
The blue eggs in the robin's nest
Will soon have wings and beak and breast,
   And flutter and fly away.

Now southward through the air I glide,
The song my only pursuivant,
And see across the landscape wide
The blue Charente, upon whose tide
The belfries and the spires of Saintes
Ripple and rock from side to side,
As, when an earthquake rends its walls,
A crumbling city reels and falls.

Who is it in the suburbs here,
This Potter, working with such cheer,
In this mean house, this mean attire,
His manly features bronzed with fire,
Whose figulines and rustic wares
Scarce find him bread from day to day?
This madman, as the people say,

Who breaks his tables and his chairs
To feed his furnace fires, nor cares
Who goes unfed if they are fed,
Nor who may live if they are dead?
This alchemist with hollow cheeks
And sunken, searching eyes, who seeks,
By mingled earths and ores combined
With potency of fire, to find
Some new enamel, hard and bright,
His dream, his passion, his delight?

O Palissy! within thy breast
Burned the hot fever of unrest;
Thine was the prophet's vision, thine
The exultation, the divine
Insanity of noble minds,
That never falters nor abates,
But labours and endures and waits,
Till all that it foresees it finds,
Or what it cannot find creates!

Turn, turn, my wheel! This earthen jar
A touch can make, a touch can mar;
*   And shall it to the Potter say,*
What makest thou? Thou hast no hand?
As men who think to understand
A world by their Creator planned,
*   Who wiser is than they.*

Still guided by the dreamy song,
As in a trance I float along
Above the Pyrenean chain,
Above the fields and farms of Spain,
Above the bright Majorcan isle,
That lends its softened name to art, –
A spot, a dot upon the chart,
Whose little towns red-roofed with tile,
Are ruby-lustred with the light
Of blazing furnaces by night,
And crowned by day with wreaths of smoke.

Then eastward, wafted in my flight
On my enchanter's magic cloak,
I sail across the Tyrrhene Sea
Into the land of Italy,
And o'er the windy Apennines,
Mantled and musical with pines.

The palaces, the princely halls,
The doors of houses and the walls
Of churches and of belfry towers,
Cloister and castle, street and mart,
Are garlanded and gay with flowers
That blossom in the fields of art.
Here Gubbio's workshops gleam and glow
With brilliant, iridescent dyes,
The dazzling whiteness of the snow,
The cobalt blue of summer skies;
And vase and scutcheon, cup and plate,
In perfect finish emulate
Faenza, Florence, Pesaro.

Forth from Urbino's gate there came
A youth with the angelic name
Of Raphael, in form and face
Himself angelic, and divine
In arts of colour and design.
From him Francesco Xanto caught
Something of his transcendent grace,
And into fictile fabrics wrought
Suggestions of the master's thought.
Nor less Maestro Giorgio shines
With madre-perl and golden lines
Of arabesques, and interweaves
His birds and fruits and flowers and leaves
About some landscape, shaded brown,
With olive tints on rock and town.
Behold this cup within whose bowl,
Upon a ground of deepest blue
With yellow-lustred stars o'erlaid,
Colours of every tint and hue

Mingle in one harmonious whole!
With large blue eyes and steadfast gaze,
Her yellow hair in net and braid,
Necklace and earrings all ablaze
With golden lustre o'er the glaze,
A woman's portrait; on the scroll,
Cana, the Beautiful! A name
Forgotten save for such brief fame
As this memorial can bestow, –
A gift some lover long ago
Gave with his heart to this fair dame.

A nobler title to renown
Is thine, O pleasant Tuscan town,
Seated beside the Arno's stream;
For Lucca della Robbia there
Created forms so wondrous fair,
They made thy sovereignty supreme.
These choristers with lips of stone,
Whose music is not heard, but seen,
Still chant, as from their organ-screen,
Their Maker's praise; nor these alone,
But the more fragile forms of clay,
Hardly less beautiful than they,
These saints and angels that adorn
The walls of hospitals, and tell
The story of good deeds so well
That poverty seems less forlorn,
And life more like a holiday.

Here in this old neglected church,
That long eludes the traveller's search,
Lies the dead bishop on his tomb;
Earth upon earth he slumbering lies,
Life-like and death-like in the gloom;
Garlands of fruit and flowers in bloom
And foliage deck his resting place;
A shadow in the sightless eyes,
A pallor on the patient face,
Made perfect by the furnace heat;

All earthly passions and desires
Burnt out by purgatorial fires;
Seeming to say, 'Our years are fleet,
And to the weary death is sweet.'

But the most wonderful of all
The ornaments on tomb and wall
That grace the fair Ausonian shores
Are those the faithful earth restores,
Near some Apulian town concealed,
In vineyard or in harvest field, –
Vases and urns and bas-reliefs,
Memorials of forgotten griefs,
Or records of heroic deeds
Of demigods and mighty chiefs:
Figures that almost move and speak,
And, buried amid mould and weeds,
Still in their attitudes attest
The presence of the graceful Greek, –
Achilles in his armour dressed,
Alcides with the Cretan bull,
And Aphrodite with her boy,
Or lovely Helena of Troy,
Still living and still beautiful.

Turn, turn, my wheel! 'Tis Nature's plan
The child should grow into the man,
*   The man grow wrinkled, old, and gray;*
In youth the heart exults and sings,
The pulses leap, the feet have wings;
In age the cricket chirps, and brings
*   The harvest home of day.*

And now the winds that southward blow,
And cool the hot Sicilian isle,
Bear me away. I see below
The long line of the Libyan Nile,
Flooding and feeding the parched land
With annual ebb and overflow,
A fallen palm whose branches lie
Beneath the Abyssinian sky,

Whose roots are in Egyptian sands.
On either bank huge water-wheels,
Belted with jars and dripping weeds,
Send forth their melancholy moans,
As if, in their gray mantles hid,
Dead anchorites of the Thebaid
Knelt on the shore and told their beads,
Beating their breasts with loud appeals
And penitential tears and groans.

This city, walled and thickly set
With glittering mosque and minaret,
Is Cairo, in whose gay bazaars
The dreaming traveller first inhales
The perfume of Arabian gales,
And sees the fabulous earthen jars,
Huge as were those wherein the maid
Morgiana found the Forty Thieves
Concealed in midnight ambuscade;
And seeing, more than half believes
The fascinating tales that run
Through all the Thousand Nights and One,
Told by the fair Scheherezade.

More strange and wonderful than these
Are the Egyptian deities,
Ammon, and Emeth, and the grand
Osiris, holding in his hand
The lotus; Isis, crowned and veiled;
The sacred Ibis, and the Sphinx;
Bracelets with blue enamelled links;
The Scarabee in emerald mailed,
Or spreading wide his funeral wings;
Lamps that perchance their night-watch kept
O'er Cleopatra while she slept, –
All plundered from the tombs of kings.

Turn, turn, my wheel! The human race
Of every tongue, of every place,
  Caucasian, Coptic, or Malay,

All that inhabit this great earth,
Whatever be their rank or worth,
Are kindred and allied by birth,
  And made of the same clay.

O'er desert sands, o'er gulf and bay,
O'er Ganges and o'er Himalay,
Bird-like I fly, and flying sing,
To flowery kingdoms of Cathay,
And bird-like poise on balanced wing
Above the town of King-te-tching,
A burning town, or seeming so, –
Three thousand furnaces that glow
Incessantly, and fill the air
With smoke uprising, gyre on gyre,
And painted by the lurid glare,
Of jets and flashes of red fire.

As leaves that in the autumn fall,
Spotted and veined with various hues,
Are swept along the avenues,
And lie in heaps by hedge and wall,
So from this grove of chimneys whirled
To all the markets of the world,
These porcelain leaves are wafted on, –
Light yellow leaves with spots and stains
Of violet and of crimson dye,
Or tender azure of a sky
Just washed by gentle April rains,
And beautiful with celadon.

Nor less the coarser household wares, –
The willow pattern, that we knew
In childhood, with its bridge of blue
Leading to unknown thoroughfares;
The solitary man who stares
At the white river flowing through
Its arches, the fantastic trees
And wild perspective of the view;
And intermingled among these

The tiles that in our nurseries
Filled us with wonder and delight,
Or haunted us in dreams at night.

And yonder by Nankin, behold!
The Tower of Porcelain, strange and old,
Uplifting to the astonished skies
Its ninefold painted balconies,
With balustrades of twining leaves,
And roofs of tile, beneath whose eaves
Hang porcelain bells that all the time
Ring with a soft, melodious chime;
While the whole fabric is ablaze
With varied tints, all fused in one
Great mass of colour, like a maze
Of flowers illumined by the sun.

Turn, turn, my wheel! What is begun
At daybreak must at dark be done,
    To-morrow will be another day;
To-morrow the hot furnace flame
Will search the heart and try the frame,
And stamp with honour or with shame
    These vessels made of clay.

Cradled and rocked in Eastern seas,
The islands of the Japanese
Beneath me lie; o'er lake and plain
The stork, the heron, and the crane
Through the clear realms of azure drift;
And on the hillside I can see
The villages of Imari,
Whose thronged and flaming workshops lift
Their twisted columns of smoke on high,
Cloud cloisters that in ruins lie,
With sunshine streaming through each rift,
And broken arches of blue sky.

All the bright flowers that fill the land,
Ripple of waves on rock or sand,

The snow on Fusiyama's cone,
The midnight heaven so thickly sown
With constellations of bright stars,
The leaves that rustle, the reeds that make
A whisper by each stream and lake,
The saffron dawn, the sunset red,
Are painted on these lovely jars;
Again the skylark sings, again
The stork, the heron, and the crane
Float through the azure overhead,
The counterfeit and counterpart
Of Nature reproduced in Art.

Art is the child of Nature; yes,
Her darling child, in whom we trace
The features of the mother's face,
Her aspect and her attitude,
All her majestic loveliness
Chastened and softened and subdued
Into a more attractive grace,
And with a human sense imbued.
He is the greatest artist, then,
Whether of pencil or of pen,
Who follows Nature. Never man,
As artist or as artisan,
Pursuing his own fantasies,
Can touch the human heart, or please,
Or satisfy our nobler needs,
As he who sets his willing feet
In Nature's footprints, light and fleet,
And follows fearless where she leads.

Thus mused I on that morn in May,
Wrapped in my visions like the Seer,
Whose eyes behold not what is near,
But only what is far away,
When, suddenly sounding peal on peal,
The church-bell from the neighbouring town
Proclaimed the welcome hour of noon.
The Potter heard, and stopped his wheel,

His apron on the grass threw down,
Whistled his quiet little tune,
Not overloud nor overlong,
And ended thus his simple song:

Stop, stop, my wheel! Too soon, too soon
The noon will be the afternoon,
*   Too soon to-day be yesterday;*
Behind us in our path we cast
The broken potsherds of the past,
And all are ground to dust at last,
*   And trodden into clay!*

Dedication

To G. W. G.

With favouring winds, o'er sunlit seas,
We sailed for the Hesperides,
The land where golden apples grow;
But that, ah! that was long ago.

How far, since then, the ocean streams
Have swept us from that land of dreams,
That land of fiction and of truth,
The lost Atlantis of our youth!

Whither, ah, whither? Are not these
The tempest-haunted Hebrides,
Where sea-gulls scream, and breakers roar
And wreck and seaweed line the shore?

Ultima Thule! Utmost Isle!
Here in thy harbours for a while
We lower our sails; a while we rest
From the unending, endless quest.

Becalmed

Becalmed upon the sea of Thought,
Still unattained the land is sought,
My mind, with loosely-hanging sails,
Lies waiting the auspicious gales.

On either side, behind, before,
The ocean stretches like a floor, –
A level floor of amethyst,
Crowned by a golden dome of mist.

Blow, breath of inspiration, blow!
Shake and uplift this golden glow!
And fill the canvas of the mind
With wafts of thy celestial wind.

Blow, breath of song! until I feel
The straining sail, the lifting keel,
The life of the awakening sea,
Its motion and its mystery!

Chimes

Sweet chimes! that in the loneliness of night
　　Salute the passing hour, and in the dark
　　And silent chambers of the household mark
　　The movements of the myriad orbs of light!
Through my closed eyelids, by the inner sight,
　　I see the constellations in the arc
　　Of their great circles moving on, and hark!
　　I almost hear them singing in their flight.
Better than sleep it is to lie awake
　　O'er-canopied by the vast starry dome
　　Of the immeasurable sky; to feel
The slumbering world sink under us, and make
　　Hardly an eddy, – a mere rush of foam
　　On the great sea beneath a sinking keel.

Four by the Clock

Four by the clock! and yet not day;
But the great world rolls and wheels away,
With its cities on land, and its ships at sea,
Into the dawn that is to be!

Only the lamp in the anchored bark
Sends its glimmer across the dark,
And the heavy breathing of the sea
Is the only sound that comes to me.

A Fragment

Awake! arise! the hour is late!
　　Angels are knocking at thy door!
They are in haste and cannot wait,
　　And once departed come no more.

Awake! arise! the athlete's arm
　　Loses its strength by too much rest;
The fallow land, the untilled farm,
　　Produces only weeds at best.

Possibilities

Where are the Poets, unto whom belong
   The Olympian heights; whose singing shafts were sent
   Straight to the mark, and not from bows half bent,
   But with the utmost tension of the thong?
Where are the stately argosies of song,
   Whose rushing keels made music as they went
   Sailing in search of some new continent,
   With all sail set, and steady winds and strong?
Perhaps there lives some dreamy boy, untaught
   In schools, some graduate of the field or street,
   Who shall become a master of the art,
An admiral sailing the high seas of thought,
   Fearless and first and steering with his fleet
   For lands not yet laid down in any chart.

The Slave's Dream

Beside the ungathered rice he lay,
    His sickle in his hand;
His breast was bare, his matted hair
    Was buried in the sand.
Again, in the mist and shadow of sleep,
    He saw his Native Land.

Wide through the landscape of his dreams
    The lordly Niger flowed;
Beneath the palm-trees on the plain
    Once more a king he strode;
And heard the tinkling caravans
    Descend the mountain-road.

He saw once more his dark-eyed queen
    Among her children stand;
They clasped his neck, they kissed his cheeks,
    They held him by the hand! –
A tear burst from the sleeper's lids
    And fell into the sand.

And then at furious speed he rode
    Along the Niger's bank;
His bridle-reins were golden chains,
    And, with a martial clank,
At each leap he could feel his scabbard of steel
    Smiting his stallion's flank.

Before him, like a blood-red flag,
    The bright flamingoes flew;
From morn till night he followed their flight,
    O'er plains where the tamarind grew,
Till he saw the roofs of Caffre huts,
    And the ocean rose to view.

At night he heard the lion roar,
    And the hyena scream,

And the river-horse, as he crushed the reeds
    Beside some hidden stream;
And it passed, like a glorious roll of drums,
    Through the triumph of his dream.

The forests, with their myriad tongues,
    Shouted of liberty;
And the Blast of the Desert cried aloud,
    With a voice so wild and free,
That he started in his sleep and smiled
    At their tempestuous glee.

He did not feel the driver's whip,
    Nor the burning heat of day;
For Death had illumined the Land of Sleep,
    And his lifeless body lay
A worn-out fetter, that the soul
    Had broken and thrown away!

Mezzo Cammin

Written at Boppard, on the Rhine,
August 25, 1842, just before leaving for home.

Half of my life is gone, and I have let
    The years slip from me and have not fulfilled
    The aspiration of my youth, to build
    Some tower of song with lofty parapet.
Not indolence, nor pleasure, nor the fret
    Of restless passions that would not be stilled,
    But sorrow, and a care that almost killed,
    Kept me from what I may accomplish yet;
Though, half-way up the hill, I see the Past
    Lying beneath me with its sounds and sights, –
    A city in the twilight dim and vast,
With smoking roofs, soft bells, and gleaming lights, –
    And hear above me on the autumnal blast
The cataract of Death far thundering from the heights.

The Cross of Snow

In the long, sleepless watches of the night,
　　A gentle face – the face of one long dead –
　　Looks at me from the wall, where round its head
　　The night-lamp casts a halo of pale light.
Here in this room she died; and soul more white
　　Never through martyrdom of fire was led
　　To its repose: nor can in books be read
　　The legend of a life more benedight.
There is a mountain in the distant West
　　That, sun-defying, in its deep ravines
　　Displays a cross of snow upon its side.
Such is the cross I wear upon my breast
　　These eighteen years, through all the changing scenes
　　And seasons, changeless since the day she died.

Chaucer

An old man in a lodge within a park;
   The chamber walls depicted all around
   With portraitures of huntsman, hawk, and hound,
  And the hurt deer. He listeneth to the lark,
Whose song comes with the sunshine through the dark
   Of painted glass in leaden lattice bound;
   He listeneth and he laugheth at the sound,
  Then writeth in a book like any clerk.
He is the poet of the dawn, who wrote
   The Canterbury Tales, and his old age
   Made beautiful with song; and as I read
I hear the crowing cock, I hear the note
   Of lark and linnet, and from every page
   Rise odours of ploughed field or flowery mead.

The Tides

I saw the long line of the vacant shore,
  The sea-weed and the shells upon the sand,
  And the brown rocks left bare on every hand,
  As if the ebbing tide would flow no more.
Then heard I, more distinctly than before,
  The ocean breathe and its great breast expand,
  And hurrying came on the defenceless land
  The insurgent waters with tumultuous roar.
All thought and feeling and desire, I said,
  Love, laughter, and the exultant joy of song
  Have ebbed from me for ever! Suddenly o'er me
They swept again from their deep ocean bed,
  And in a tumult of delight, and strong
  As youth, and beautiful as youth, upbore me.

A Nameless Grave

'A soldier of the Union mustered out,'
 Is the inscription on an unknown grave
 At Newport News, beside the salt-sea wave,
 Nameless and dateless; sentinel or scout
Shot down in skirmish, or disastrous rout
 Of battle, when the loud artillery drave
 Its iron wedges through the ranks of brave
 And doomed battalions, storming the redoubt.
Thou unknown hero sleeping by the sea
 In thy forgotten grave! with secret shame
 I feel my pulses beat, my forehead burn,
When I remember thou hast given for me
 All that thou hadst, thy life, thy very name,
 And I can give thee nothing in return.

The Tide Rises, the Tide Falls

The tide rises, the tide falls,
The twilight darkens, the curlew calls;
Along the sea-sands damp and brown
The traveller hastens toward the town,
    And the tide rises, the tide falls.

Darkness settles on roofs and walls,
But the sea in the darkness calls and calls;
The little waves, with their soft white hands,
Efface the footprints in the sands,
    And the tide rises, the tide falls.

The morning breaks; the steeds in their stalls
Stamp and neigh, as the hostler calls;
The day returns, but nevermore
Returns the traveller to the shore,
    And the tide rises, the tide falls.

L'Envoi

Ye voices, that arose
After the Evening's close,
And whispered to my restless heart repose!

Go, breathe it in the ear
Of all who doubt and fear,
And say to them, 'Be of good cheer!'

Ye sounds, so low and calm,
That in the groves of balm
Seemed to me like an angel's psalm!

Go, mingle yet once more
With the perpetual roar
Of the pine forest, dark and hoar!

Tongues of the dead, not lost,
But speaking from death's frost,
Like fiery tongues at Pentecost!

Glimmer, as funeral lamps,
Amid the chills and damps
Of the vast plain where Death encamps!

Everyman's Poetry

Titles available in this series **all at £1.00**

William Blake
ed. Peter Butter
0 460 87800 X

Robert Burns
ed. Donald Low
0 460 87814 X

Samuel Taylor Coleridge
ed. John Beer
0 460 87826 3

Thomas Gray
ed. Robert Mack
0 460 87805 0

Ivor Gurney
ed. George Walter
0 460 87797 6

George Herbert
ed. D. J. Enright
0 460 87795 X

Robert Herrick
ed. Douglas Brooks-Davies
0 460 87799 2

John Keats
ed. Nicholas Roe
0 460 87808 5

**Henry Wadsworth
Longfellow**
ed. Anthony Thwaite
0 460 87821 2

John Milton
ed. Gordon Campbell
0 460 87813 1

Edgar Allan Poe
ed. Richard Gray
0 460 87804 2

Poetry Please!
Foreword by Charles
Causley
0 460 87824 7

Alexander Pope
ed. Douglas Brooks-Davies
0 460 87798 4

Lord Rochester
ed. Paddy Lyons
0 460 87819 0

Christina Rossetti
ed. Jan Marsh
0 460 87820 4

William Shakespeare
ed. Martin Dodsworth
0 460 87815 8

Alfred, Lord Tennyson
ed. Michael Baron
0 460 87802 6

R. S. Thomas
ed. Anthony Thwaite
0 460 87811 5

Walt Whitman
ed. Ellman Crasnow
0 460 87825 5

Oscar Wilde
ed. Robert Mighall
0 460 87803 4